THE SUN GOD'S CHILDREN

James Willard Schultz
and
Jessie Louise Donaldson

RIVERBEND
PUBLISHING

The Sun God's Children

Copyright © 2010 by the Museum of the Rockies

Published by Riverbend Publishing, Helena, Montana, in cooperation with the Museum of the Rockies, Bozeman, Montana

The Sun God's Children was first published in 1930.

ISBN: 978-1-60639-022-1

Printed in the United States of America.

2 3 4 5 6 7 8 9 0 SB 20 19 18 17 16 15 14

Cover design by DD Dowden

Text design by Suzan Glosser

Front cover photo and credit:
Blackfeet warrior (probably Big Moon) on his warhorse, Cutbank valley, Montana, buffalo skull in the foreground, circa 1900. A handcolored lantern slide by Walter McClintock (1870-1946), Yale Collection of Western Americana, Beinecke Rare Book and Manuscript Library.

Back cover photo credit: T. J. Hileman, Minnesota Historical Society

RIVERBEND PUBLISHING
P.O. Box 5833
Helena, MT 59604
1-866-787-2363
www.riverbendpublishing.com

TABLE OF CONTENTS

INTRODUCTION

By Darrell Robes Kipp
Executive Director of the Piegan Institute
Browning, Montana

In 1944, a few days after I was born, my grandmother gave me the name, Apiniokio Peta, Morning Eagle, the honored name of her uncle. My grandmother's English name was Mary Kipp, and she was the wife of Sequeenamakah, Last Gun, who appeared in one of James Willard Schultz's books as Makapini, or Red Eyes. A survivor of the infamous Baker Massacre on the Bear River in 1870, Last Gun, whose English name was Richard Kipp, grew up in the household of Joseph Kipp, one of the army scouts involved in the massacre. Perhaps in part to repair his reputation among the Blackfeet tribe, Kipp took in a number of children orphaned in the massacre and later married one of them, Last Gun's sister Double Strike Woman. Joseph Kipp, whom Schultz calls Berry in his books, was one of the first friends Schultz made after arriving in Fort Benton in 1877, and many of Schultz's tales originate from their close association. Certainly, then, my grandfather, who grew up in Kipp's household, knew Schultz well as did my grandmother and their children.

I remember, as a child, listening to my father, Thomas Kipp, tell us his father's stories from the days when Last Gun hauled freight in horse drawn wagons for Joseph Kipp. In the fashion of children listening to their parents' stories, I seldom connected them to the greater story of the tribe, and it was not until years later, when I began to read Schultz's books, did I discover the various connections between our family and Schultz's life among the Blackfeet.

James Willard Shultz came among the Blackfeet in a pivotal period: the end of the buffalo hunting days for all plains tribes, including the Blackfeet, occurred less than ten years after his arrival in Montana. The Blackfeet were people of the buffalo, and much of their life ways derived from their relationship with the buffalo herds. It is safe to say that the tribe faced great disorder and misfortune following the buffalo's demise.

Much has been written about the status of Indians since then, with many chroniclers insisting that "real" Indians ceased to exist once the buffalo hunting days were over. This is a slap in the face to Indians living today, and I among them cringe at such statements. One of the reasons I like Schultz's work is that he never puts Indians away as relics of a past era, but through his storytelling keeps the old days fresh in his reader's mind.

The idea that modern Indians are somehow not "real" Indians continues to exist today. It is, of course, a very ethnocentric viewpoint, and if applied to American society in general would lead to the view that there are no "real" Americans left in this country, for just as Indians' circumstances have changed over the last two hundred years, so have the circumstances of their white counterparts. Among the Blackfeet, introduction of horses, guns, and, for that matter, steel, automobiles, and computers has marked the end of various earlier epochs, but the tribe's bonds have remained strong, as has a continuing appreciation among tribal members for timeless stories about our history, and how our people have adapted to these changes. Today, Indians seek knowledge of their past just like any other group, and Schultz's work serves their purpose well.

My fellow tribal members who enjoy Schultz's books give him high marks for storytelling and for keeping memories alive. While some purists scoff at the way he romanticized our tribal history, most of us rejoice in his recollections. We especially rejoice because he was so prolific, and his stories cover the gamut of the tribe's trials and tribulations, as well as our oral tradition.

Some have criticized Schultz for placing himself in his stories at the expense of objectivity. I would argue, in fact, that this is one of his strengths as a writer. He could put himself into the story as easily as he put the reader into it. While his work doesn't meet academic standards of objectivity, it isn't dry and pedantically academic, either. Others have questioned Schultz's competence in speaking the Blackfeet language. Certainly, however, he communicated well in the language, as well as in sign language, and this is reflected in his writings. (After all, his wife Natahki did not speak English, nor did most of tribal members Schultz knew during the time he lived among them.) This fact alone separates him from most of the other chroniclers of the Blackfeet people: he spoke the language and, through his marriage to Natahki, had access to all their inner sanctum settings, as well daily life trials and tribulation. (It is important to understand that marriage within the tribe was viewed first and foremost as an alliance and marked the taking on of an ally, so Schultz's marriage was viewed, by members of the tribe as a significant connection.)

In addition to having access to tribal stories and rituals, Schultz also had access to white trappers and traders known to the tribe such as James Bird, Charles Rivois, Joe Kipp, and the venerated Hugh Monroe (Rising Wolf). These men were a virtual library of Blackfeet lore, and they, like Schultz, understood the basic rule of Blackfeet storytelling: truth. For among the Blackfeet, the primary element in how they honored the Creator's work derived from truthfulness. A story without truth was considered an insult to the listeners. So, although Schultz sometimes used poetic license in addressing his literary audiences, it was unlikely he could bring himself to roam too far afield without trepidation. Schultz's detractors balk at his sweeping judgments, his inexact and inconsistent chronology, and his renaming of characters, but in all, as a tribal member, I have no reason not to rely on his work as recollections of someone who was there. Other informed tribal members confirm my perspective and praise the authenticity of Schultz's descriptions of various Blackfeet ceremonies.

Schultz's intimacy with the Blackfeet extended to his intimacy with Glacier National Park. As his biographer Warren L. Hanna, states in *The Life and Times of James Willard Schultz (APikúni)*, "I am satisfied that no one has done more to make the park beloved, as well as famous, than James Willard Schultz." In fact, Schultz helped discover—and promote—many of the park's major attractions, if the word "discover" is used to mean "discover by non-Indians." The oral tradition of the tribe fully chronicles the glaciers, lakes, mountains, streams, and trails of the area with long-established Blackfeet names and descriptions. From these tribal traditions, Schultz undoubtedly had learned a great deal about the area before he actually traveled it with the George Bird Grinnell in 1884. Schultz certainly influenced the naming of various topographical elements in the area, though many of his names echoed names taught to him by the Blackfeet people.

The establishment of the park was the dream of writer and editor of *Forest and Stream* George Bird Grinnell, who viewed it as a scheme worthy of taking up with Louis Hill, president of the Great Northern Railway. Hill helped push Congress to authorize the park in 1910 and then worked hard to promote it as a tourist destination—with the expectation that the tourists would travel there via his railroad. Schultz remained beholden to both Grinnell and Hill because they purchased his writings, and he often made it clear to them he would write what they wanted. These offers have put Schultz's reputation for accuracy in jeopardy, yet the fact that Schultz wrote for mercenary reasons should not necessarily discredit his stories.

Ultimately, Schultz's place among the Blackfeet tribe was one of long-term friend and fellow traveler. His marriage to a Blackfeet woman connected him to the tribe, and the birth of his son, Hart Merriam Schultz, or Lone Wolf, strengthened that connection. In 1985, during my early work as a language researcher among my tribe, there still were individuals who remembered Schultz personally, and their recollections were of a man who lived with them and was accepted as part of the tribe. His burial by the tribe near Two Medicine River is testament to his acceptance and strong alliance.

Academics find it easy to criticize in Schultz for his romanticism, lack of objectivity, and casual scholarship, but in my view his strengths outweigh his flaws. A prolific, excellent storyteller, he presented the essence of the Blackfeet tribe as no other writer was able to then or has since.

*Dedicated to the memory of
W. R. Mills, or Pita Kishtsipi (Striped Eagle)
as his Blackfeet friends
so lovingly named him
in the long-ago*

PREFACE

The "Warlike Blackfeet," one time terror of white trappers and adventurers, dread enemies of other Plains tribes, and of Mountain tribes, we have chosen to call "The Sun God's Children." For those of us who know the Blackfeet intimately—have lived with them in their lodges, gone on the war trail with their fearless youth, experienced the glow, the beauty of their beliefs and ceremonies—recognize them as a people devoted to their homes and families, honorable in their dealings with their fellow men, proud, courageous, and reverent worshippers of the sun. Until advancing hordes of emigrants hemmed them in, theirs was a vast domain of mountains, grassy plains, and wide, timbered valleys. With game in plenty, they knew not want. Choicest of food was fat buffalo meat; warmest of coverings, soft tanned buffalo robes; most comfortable of homes, the lodges of tanned buffalo leather: Sun's gifts, all of them, to his favored children.

To integrate the activities of the life of the Blackfeet tribes, in the days of the buffalo, and including certain of their ceremonials of the present time, is the purpose of this book. Particularly, it is written in response to the request of so many sojourners in Glacier National Park and Waterton Lakes National Park, who have there spent many pleasant hours in the camps of members of these tribes, have become greatly interested in them, and desire to know more of the inner life of these, the Sun God's Children.

The Authors
Waterton Lakes National Park
Alberta, September 1, 1929

A pictograph by Many Big Ears of his encounter with the Crows (top) and a large buffalo bull (lower).

CHAPTER I

WHEN FIRST MET BY THE FUR-TRADERS

OF the fifty-six distinct linguistic stocks of Indians in North America, the Algonquian was the largest, embracing as it did forty-nine tribes, inhabiting the northern United States and Canada from the Rocky Mountains to the Gulf of St. Lawrence, and thence south along the Atlantic Coast into Delaware. Of these Algonquins, the three tribes of Blackfeet, and their allies, the Gros Ventres (also Algonquian), were the westernmost. When first met by white men, these four tribes controlled an extent of country more vast, far more vast, than was dominated by any other tribe or allied tribes of Indians. It extended from the North Saskatchewan River, in Alberta, south for six hundred miles to the Yellowstone River, and from the Rocky Mountains, between these two rivers, eastward upon the plains for an average distance of nearly four hundred miles.

It is uncertain who were the white men who first met the Blackfeet tribes. They were, most likely, the sons of Sieur Pierre Gaultier de Varennes de la Verendrie, who built a post, Fort Poskoyac, at the forks of the Saskatchewan River, in 1739. They may have been the ten Canadians (French) who, at the instance of the Chevalier de Niverville, ascended the North or the South Branch of the Saskatchewan, in 1751, and 'established a post near the Rocky Mountains,' only to abandon it in the following spring. Again, it may have been that the first whites the Blackfeet saw were Spaniards, for, even before the time of the Verendries, war parties of them went to raid the horse herds of those early settlers in the Southwest, leaving their own country in the spring and returning to it in the summer of the following year. As late as the 1870s, there were in the possession of the Pikû´ni tribe of the Blackfeet, a Toledo blade, a shirt of mail, and a lance that had been taken from the Spaniards in those far-back raids.

Prior to the advent of the horse in the Far Northwest, the Blackfeet tribes, and their close allies, the Gros Ventres, roamed about in a stretch of country extending from the Rocky Mountains east to the Forks of the Saskatchewan, and from the South Fork northward to the headwaters of the Athabaska River. We may take it, however, that they lived mainly upon the northern border of the Saskatchewan plains, living principally upon the meat of the buffalo, most plentiful and most easily obtainable of all the game animals of that country. Their nearest neighbors on the north and east were the Crees, also Algonquins, and the Assiniboins, of Siouan stock. Yet so long had they lived apart from the Crees that neither tribe could understand the other, although the grammatical structure of the two languages remained the same. And still more changed, and more difficult, was the language of the Algonquian Gros Ventres. Neither Blackfeet nor Cree ever attempted to master it. The Blackfeet were so proud that. they, as they said, would not demean themselves by learning a foreign language. Many of the members of the Crees and the Gros Ventres, however, spoke the Blackfeet language fluently.

The first white man to penetrate the country of the Blackfeet and to write his impressions of them was Anthony Hendry, of the Hudson's Bay Company.[1] He left its York Factory, on Hudson Bay, in the spring of 1754, with a flotilla (canoes manned by the 'natives' of that section, Ojibways and Crees, with their families, and on Sunday, September 29 of that year, met some members of one or another of the Blackfeet tribes, as he called

---

[1] York Factory to the Blackfeet Country: The Journal of Anthony Hendry, 1754-1755. Edited by Lawrence J. Burpee. Proceedings and Transactions of the Royal Society of Canada, 1907, 3d Series, vol. 1.

them, Archithinues,[1] a few miles north of the present city of Calgary. The Crees and Ojibways had not then obtained (horses; they traveled about with canoes or on foot, with dogs for their beasts of burden; but the Blackfeet, Hendry found, were the owners of great numbers of horses. It is probable that they obtained the beginnings of their herds as early as the year 1700. Hendry called the buffalo-leather lodges of the Blackfeet, tents, as did later adventuring fur-traders who penetrated their country. The entry in his 'Journal' for October 14, is as follows:

October 14. 4 men, Archithinue natives, on horseback sent to find whether we are friends or enemies We told them friends. Came to 200 tents of Archithinue natives pitched in two rows, and an opening in the middle, where we were conducted to the Leader's tent; which was at one end, large enough to accommodate 50 persons. He received us seated on a clear [white] buffalo skin, attended by 20 elderly men. He made signs for me to sit on his right hand, which I did. Our leader set up several grand-pipes and smoked all around, according to the usual custom; not a word was yet spoke on either side. Smoking being over, Buffalo flesh boiled was served round in a species of bent, and I was presented with 10 Buffalo tongues....

October 15. Tuesday. About 10 o'clock A.M. I was invited to the Archithinue's tent; when by an interpreter I told him what I was sent for,

---

[1]Archithinues was Hendry's, and later adventurers' attempt to spell the sound of the Ojibway name for the Blackfeet tribe Aiahkiniwuk — Strange People. There is no sound of *r* in Ojibway, Chippewa, and Cree, nor in the Blackfeet language.

and desired of him to allow some of his young men to go down to the Fort with me where they would be kindly received and get guns &c. But he answered it was too far off, and they could not live without buffalo flesh; and that they could not leave their horses &c; and many other obstacles, though all might be gotten over if they were acquainted with a canoe, and could eat fish, which they never do. The chief further said that they never wanted food, as they followed the buffalo and killed them with the bows and arrows; and he was informed that the natives who frequented the settlements, were oftentimes starved on the journey. Such remarks I thought exceeding true. He made me a present of a handsome bow and arrows, and in return I gave him a part of each kind of goods I had, as ordered by Mr. Isham's written instructions. I departed and took a good view of the camp. Their tents were pitched close together in two regular lines, which formed a broad street open at both ends. Their horses were turned out to grass, their legs being fettered; and when wanted are fastened to lines cut of buffalo skin, that stretches along and is fastened to stakes drove in the ground. They have their hair halters, Buffalo skin pads and stirrups of the same. The horses are fine tractable animals about 14 hands high, being lively and clean made. The natives are good horsemen and kill the buffalo on them. These natives are dressed much the same as the others; but are more clean and Sprightly. They think nothing of my tobacco, and I set little value upon theirs, which is dried horse dung.... Saw many *fine girls who were captives*, and a great many dried scalps with fine long black hair, displayed on poles before the leader's tent. They follow the buffalo from place to place; and that they should not be surprised by the enemy, encamp in the open plains. Their fuel is turf, and horse dung dryed; their clothing is finely painted with red paints like the English ochre; but *they do not mark nor paint their bodies*. Saw four asses.

May 16. 30 miles N. Came to 30 tents of Archithinue Natives. I talked with them as I did to the others; but all to no purpose. Our Indians traded a great many furs from them. They have the

15

finest horses I have yet seen here and are a very *kind people*.

May 21. 70 tents of Archithinue Natives came to us, headed by the Leader that I saw in the Muscoty country. I used my utmost endeavours to get a few of the young men to the Fort, but all to no purpose. They have very few Wolves or Furs of any kind, having traded them to the Pegoganaw Indians, who are gone to the fort. We are about 60 canoes and there are scarce a Gun, Kettle, Hatchet or Knife amongst us, having traded them with the Archithinue Natives.

The above was the last entry in his 'Journal' about the Blackfeet. He returned to York Factory without having induced them to go there to trade. They had no reason to go there, as it is clearly shown in the 'Journal' that the 'natives' who traded at York Factory annually made the long journey up the Saskatchewan to supply them with white men's good in exchange for their furs.

We learn from Hendry's notes that, in 1754, the Blackfeet owned many horses, and many slaves, female slaves particularly; that they were nomadic and successful buffalo hunters; that they were fairly friendly terms with the Assiniboins, with whom they were later on to be constantly at war. Hendry was mistaken in several of his observations of their customs. The 'turf' fuel that he believed they used was undoubtedly dried buffalo chips, to which always clung some of the earth and the grass upon which the chips had fallen. Nor did they smoke horse dung. It is unsmokeable. They had at that time tobacco of their own planting and harvesting — *Nicotiana quadrivalvis* — as the next trader to visit them carefully noted. Lastly, we learn from Hendry's 'Journal' that the Blackfeet were, when he visited them, 'a very kind people,' and that they 'looked more like to Europeans than Indians.'

So far as is known, after Hendry, no other white man visited the Blackfeet tribes until Matthew Cocking, Second Factor at York Factory, journeyed to them in 1772, also to try to induce them to make annual pilgrimages to that post with their catches of furs. Like Hendry, he was accompanied by many canoes of 'natives,' who, instead of scattering out and trapping every winter, as the Hudson's Bay Company desired them to do, annually ascended the Saskatchewan, and, with a meager supply of kettles, knives, hatchets, vermilion, and trinkets, a few guns and powder and balls, obtained the fur catches of the Blackfeet tribes. Cocking kept a daily record of his long journey, from which I quote the following, pertaining to the Blackfeet:

October 7. I found in an old tent place belonging to the Archithinue Natives, part of an earthen vessel in which they dress their victuals. It appeared to have been in the form of an earthen pan.

October 16-19. The Natives shew me a tobacco plantation belonging to the Archithinue Natives, about 100 yards long and 5 wide, sheltered from the northern blasts by a ledge of poplars; and to the southward by a ridge of high ground....

November 4. I shall be sorry if I do not see the Equestrian Natives [Blackfeet], who are certainly a brave people, and far superior to any tribes that visit our forts; they have dealings with no Europeans, but live in a state of nature to the S. W. Westerly; draw to the N. E. in March to meet our Natives who traffic with them.

December 1. Our Archithinue friends came to us and pitched a small distance from us....This tribe is named Powestic Athinuewuck, i.e., Waterfall Indians. There are four tribes, or nations, more, which are all Equestrian Indians. viz. Mithco Athiniwuck or Bloody Indians, Koskitow Wathesitock or Black-footed Indians, Pigonow or Muddy Water Indians, and Sassewuck or Woody Country Indians.

December 3. Smoked with Archithinue Indians, tried to persuade to go to Fort. They said they would be starved and were unacquainted with canoes, and mentioned the long distance. I am certain they never can be prevailed upon to undertake such journeys.

December 4.....In all their actions they far excell the other Natives. They are all well mounted on light sprightly animals; their weapons, Bows and Arrows. Several have on jackets of moose leather 6 fold quilted and without sleeves. They likewise use pack horses; which give their women great advantage over the other women who are either carrying or hauling on sledges every day in the year. They appear to be more like Europeans than Americans.

[1]*Matthew Cocking's Journal.* Being the Journal of a journey performed by Mr. Matthew Cocking, Second Factor at York Fort, in order to take a view of the Inland Country, and to promote the Hudson's Bay Company's interests, whose trade is diminishing by the Canadians yearly intercepting natives on their way to the Settlements. 1772-1773. Royal Society of Canada, 1907, *Proceedings and Transactions,* vol. 1.

December 5. Our Archithinue friends are very hospitable, continually inviting us to partake of their best fare; generally berries infused with water with fat, very agreeable eating. Their manner of showing respect to strangers is holding the pipe while they smoke; this is done three times. Afterward every person smoked in common; the Women excepted, whom I did not observe to take the pipe. The tobacco they use is of their own planting; which hath a disagreeable flavor. I have preserved a specimen. These people are more cleanly in their clothing and food than my companions. Their victuals are dressed in earthen pots of their own manufacturing, much in the form of Newcastle pots, but without feet; their fire tackling a black stone used as a flint, and a kind of ore as steel, using tuss balls as tinder, i.e., a kind of moss....The slaves whom they have preserved alive are used with kindness; they are young people of both sexes, and are adopted into the families of those who have lost their children, either by War or sickness.

So end abruptly Cocking's notes on the Blackfeet tribes and their allies, the 'Waterfall Indians,' who were the Gros Ventres of the prairie, and the 'Woody Country Indians,' the Saksiks (Sarsees, as the Canadian Government has it), of Athapaskan stock. Interesting and valuable were his discoveries that they made earthen pots, planted tobacco gardens, and were very hospitable. And, like Hendry, he thought that they were more like Europeans than Americans.

Not long after Cocking visited the Blackfeet tribes, the Hudson's Bay Company, and a little later, its bitter rival, the Northwest Fur Company, established posts on both branches of the

Saskatchewan River, to obtain their trade. Edward Unfreville, of the latter company, who wrote 'The Present State of Hudson's Bay' (London, 1790), said of them (page 198):

The usual method of conversing with the Fall Indians [Gros Ventre] is by speaking the Blackfeet tongue, which is agreeable, and soon acquired.

(Page 200.) The Blackfeet, Blood, and Paegan Indians. These Indians, though divided into the above three tribes, are all one nation, speak the same language, and abide by the same laws and customs. For what reason they are thus denominated I have been unable to discover, but they go by no other name among the Nehethawas.[1] They are the most numerous and powerful nation we are acquainted with; and, by living on the borders of the enemies' country, are the principal barrier to prevent their incursions. War is more familiar to them than the other nations, and they are by far the most formidable to the common enemy of the whole. In their inroads into the enemies' country they frequently bring off a number of horses, which is their principal inducement in going to war.

These people are not so far enervated by the use of spirituous liquors, as to be slaves to it; when they come to trade they drink moderately and buy themselves necessities for war, and domestic conveniences. They annually bring a good quantity of skins to the traders, but a greater quantity by far of wolves. All these tribes have a custom peculiar to themselves, which is the cutting off the joints of their fingers, beginning with the little finger, and taking off a joint as often as superstition prompts them. I

[1]It should be Nahiawuk, the Cree Indians' name for themselves, meaning, 'Native People.'

have not been able to learn for certain the cause of this singular custom, nor did I observe any but the old men, who had their fingers thus mutilated.

They behave very friendly to those of our people who pass the winter with them, and none of them have as yet received any injury under their protection, either in person or effects. The people of this nation will eat no kind of waterfowl, amphibious animal, or fish. Their chief substance is the flesh of the buffalo, the deer species, and likewise vegetables. Their language is not very grateful to the ear of the stranger, but when learnt is both agreeable and expressive.

(Page 203.) Before the fatal attack of smallpox, which broke out in the year 1781, all these nations of Indians were much more numerous than they are at present....It is computed that at least one-half of the inhabitants were carried off by it.

Of all the early fur-traders who had dealings with the Blackfeet tribes, Alexander Hendry, Jr., left the most complete account of them. But he was a prejudiced observer of them and their customs. Dr. Elliott Coues, the editor of his 'Journal'[1] gives the following estimate of the man:

Intimately connected with his customers as he was, thoroughly versed in their characters, habits, and manners as he became, he had no sympathy with them whatever. They were simply the necessary nuisances of his business, against whom his antipathies were continually excited and not seldom betrayed in his narrative.

[1] *The Manuscript Journals of Alexander Henry, Fur-Trader of the Northwest Fur Company, and of David Thompson, Official Geographer and Explorer of the Same Company, 1799-1814.* Edited by Elliott Coues. New York, Francis P. Harper, 1897.

He detested an Indian as much as he despized a Franco-Canadian voyageur, or hated a rival of the Hudson's Bay Company, or X. Y. Company. How much of 'sweetness and light' is likely to seep into the pages of a man whose prejudices were invincible and sometimes violent, of one who was quite out of touch with his own environment, the reader may judge for himself.

In Chapter XIV, 'Ethnography of Fort Vermillion,' Henry wrote of the Blackfeet tribes, 'The Blackfeet, Bloods, and Piegans may be considered under one grand appellation of Slave Indians.' This term he got from his Cree and Ojibway friends, whose name for the Blackfeet tribes as a whole was — and is — Ahwa´kanek... (Slave People), for the reason that they had many slaves, captured in their wars with other tribes. There was, much farther north, on the tributaries of the Mackenzie River, a tribe of Athapaskan stock that was named Slave, or Slavey Indians, and it is probable that the earliest adventurers of the fur-traders named the Slave Lakes for them.

Henry, as well as other early fur-traders, compiled a vocabulary of the Blackfeet language, and, like the others, he gave many of the words certain sounds which no Blackfeet could possibly utter. There is absolutely no sound of the letters *b, d, f, g, j, l, r,* and *z* in their language. The following are a few examples from his vocabulary:

English	Henry	Correct Form
You	Kristoo	Ksto'ah
Go	Mistabout	Ûhko'
Throat	Ochristone	Oksîstun'
Fly	Seeskrisiss	Su'îsksiks
Naked	Kutedgeessookas	Namp'si
Rabbit	Pahkabssahme	Ah'ahchîstah

The following are a few of Henry's notes on the Blackfeet tribes:

The Piegans, though the same people as the Black-feet and Bloods, imagine themselves to be a superior race, braver and more virtuous than their own countrymen, whom they always seem to despize for their vicious habits and treacherous conduct. They are proud and haughty, and studiously avoid the company of their allies further than is necessary for their own safety in guarding against their common enemies.... They have always had the reputation of being more brave and virtuous than any of their neighbors; indeed they are obliged to be so, surrounded as they are by enemies with whom they are constantly at war....The country which the Piegans call their own, and which they have been known to inhabit since their first intercourse with traders on the Saskatchewan, is, as I have already observed, along the foot of the Rocky Mountains, on Bow River, and even as far south as the Missouri. The buffalo regulates their movements over this vast extent of prairie throughout the year, as they must keep near these animals to obtain food.

The ordinary dress of these people is plain and simple, like that of all other Meadow Indians; plain leather shoes, leather leggings reaching up to the hip, and a robe over all, constitutes their usual summer dress, though occasionally they wear an open leather shirt, which reaches down to the thigh. Their winter dress differs little from that of the summer; their shoes are then made of buffalo hide dressed in the hair, and sometimes a leather shirt and a strip of buffalo or wolf skin is tied around the head. They never wear mittens. I have frequently seen them come into our houses after a 10 or 15 days' march over the plains, in the depth of winter, with the thermometer 30 or 40 degrees below zero, dressed with only shoes, leggings, and a robe — nothing else to screen them from the cold....Young Piegans are not so much addicted to fineries as the Blackfeet; their only ambition being for war; their manners, however, are the same. The gun which they carry in their arms, the powder horn and shot-pouch slung on their backs, are necessary appendages to the full dress of a young Slave. The bow and quiver of arrows are also slung across the back at all times and seasons, except that, when the Indian is sleeping or setting in his tent, these weapons are hung on a pole within reach....War seems to be the Piegans' sole delight; their discourse always turns upon that subject; one war-party no sooner arrives than another sets off....They take great delight in relating their adventures in war, and are so vivid in rehearsing every detail of the fray that they seem to be fighting the battle over again. A Piegan takes as much pleasure in the particulars of the excursion in which he engaged as a Saulteur does in relating a grand drinking match — how many nights they were drunk and how many kegs of liquor they consumed.

In smoking there is more ceremony among the Piegans than I have observed in any other tribe.

Some of them will not smoke while there is an old pair of shoes hanging in the tent; some of them must rest the pipe upon a piece of meat; others upon a buffalo's tongue. Some will smoke only their own pipe which they themselves must light; again, others must have somebody to light it for them, and then it must be lighted by flame only; no live coal must touch it, nor must the coal be blown into a blaze. No person must pass between the fire and the lighted pipe, particularly when in a tent. The first whiff of the pipe is blown to the earth, while the stem is pointed down, or sometimes to the rising sun; the midday sun and the setting sun also receive their share of attention.

Every movement of the Slaves is a parade. When coming in to trade, young men are sent on ahead to inform us of their approach and demand a bit of tobacco for each principal man or head of a family. Six inches of our twist tobacco is commonly sent, neatly done up in paper, to which is tied a small piece of vermillion, with which they immediately return to their friends. The tobacco is delivered, and a smoking match takes place, while the messengers relate the news of the place, and give an account of their reception. This ceremony being concluded they move on their journey in one long string. On the day of their arrival the men assemble at a convenient spot in sight of the fort, where they make fire and smoke; during which time the women and children come to the fort and erect their tents near the stockades. Observing that business to be nearly completed, then men arise and move toward the fort in Indian file, the principal chief taking the lead, the others falling in according to rank or precedence, derived from the number of scalps taken in war. The master of the place is always expected to go out and shake hands with them at a short distance from the gates, and the further he goes to meet them, the greater the compliment. This ceremony over, he walks at their head, and this conducts them to the Indian hall. There he desires the principal chief to take the seat of honor, in the most conspicuous place; the others to sit according to their rank around the room on benches provided for that purpose. The pipe is then lighted and presented to the chief, who, having performed the usual ceremonies, takes a few whiffs and passes it to the next person on the right, always in rotation, with the course of the sun. All having taken a few whiffs of the trader's pipe, the principal chief produces his own, which he fills and presents to the trader, who must take a few whiffs before it is sent around. The compliment is greater if the chief presents the pipe to the trader to light. If the Indians are numerous their own pipes are then demanded, filled by us, and presented to them, each one lighting according to his own particular notions of ceremony; but we must always have people to hand them fire, as their consequential impertinence does not permit them to rise for that purpose. The more pipes there are in circulation at once, the greater is the compliment.

Some of the Blackfeet own 40 or 50 horses. But the Piegans have by far the greatest numbers; I heard of one man who had 300. These animals are got from their enemies southward, where they are perpetually at war with the Snakes, Flatheads, and other nations, who have vast herds....A common horse can be bought here for a carrot of tobacco, which weighs about three pounds, and costs in Canada four shillings. The saddles these people use are of two kinds. The one which I suppose to be of the most ancient construction is made of wood well joined, and covered with raw buffalo hide, which in drying binds every part tight. This frame rises about ten inches before and behind; the tops are bent over horizontally and spread out, forming a flat piece about six inches in diameter. The stirrup, attached to the frame by a leather thong, is a piece of bent wood, over which is stretched raw buffalo hide, making it firm and strong. When an Indian goes to mount he throws his buffalo robe over the saddle and rides on it. The other saddle, which is the same as that of the Assiniboins and Crees, is made by shaping two pieces of parchment on dressed leather, about 20 inches long and 14 broad, through the length of which are sewed two parallel lines three inches apart, on each side of which the saddle is well stuffed with moose or red deer hair. Under each kind of saddle are placed two or three folds of soft dressed buffalo skin, to keep the horse from getting a sore back.

Their tents are large and clean. The devices used in painting them are taken from beasts and birds; the buffalo and the bear are frequently delineated, but in a rude and uncouth manner. They are great warriors, and so easily prey upon their enemies that many of the old men have killed with their own hands, during their younger days, 15 or 20 men. Women and children are never reckoned; and he is considered but a moderate warrior who has killed only 10 men.

They are exceedingly superstitious in all their actions; even their smoking is done with many superstitious manouvers. Some rest their pipes on a small stone which they carry about for that purpose; others on a dry buffalo dung; others again on a particular piece of earth, clay, wood, or metal. Some of them have a small bone whistle suspended to their necks, and on taking a fresh-lighted pipe, whistle several times before they smoke, at the same time waving the hands on each side of the stem. The pipe is always passed round in rotation with the sun; and they never press down its contents with the finger after it is once lighted, a small stick being used for that purpose. Each man draws only a few whiffs, and instantly hands it to the next on his left.

The following is the present population, as nearly as I could ascertain it:

> 120 Tents, Painted Feather's band .... 360 warriors
> 80 Tents, Cold band .... 160 warriors
> 100 Tents, Bloods .... 200 warriors
> 350 Tents, Piegans or Picaneaux .... 700 warriors
> 650 Tents of Slaves, or about .... 1,420 warriors

Painted Feather's band are the most civilized, and well disposed toward us. The Cold band are notoriously a set of audacious villians. The Bloods are still worse, always inclined to mischief and murder. The Piegans are the most numerous and best disposed toward us of all the Indians of the plains. They also kill beaver. The other tribes stand in awe of them, and they have frequently offered us their services to quell disturbances made by other tribes.

The Big Bellies, or Rapid Indians, are now stationed south of the Slaves, between the South Branch [of the Saskatchewan] and the Missourie. Formerly they inhabited the point of land between the North and South branches of the Saskatchewan to the junction of those two streams; from which circumstance, it is supposed, they derived the name of Rapid Indians.... Their dress, manners and customs appear to me to be the same. [Same as the Slaves.] Formerly they were very numerous, and much dreaded by neighboring nations. But since the smallpox their numbers have diminished very much, through the effect of that baneful disease, and in consequence of depredations committed upon them by tribes with whom they have been at variance. The Slaves have fought many bloody battles with them, though they are now on amicable terms. They are a more industrious people, and commonly bring us a good trade in dried provisions, beaver skins, and grizzly bear and buffalo robes. In dressing their robes they are far superiour to the Slaves, and fully equal to the Mandanes.

They are an audacious, turbulent race, and have repeatedly attempted to massacre us. Their first attack was made at old Fort Brule in 1793, when they pillaged the Hudson's Bay Company's fort, and were about to commit a similar outrage upon that of the N. W. Co.; but, through the spirited conduct of one of the clerks, they were repulsed, and fled with the booty already acquired from the H. B. Co. establishment. The following summer they assembled and formally attacked the H. B. Co. fort on the South Branch, which they destroyed, massacred the people, and pillaged them of everything they could find, leaving the place in ashes. At the same time they attempted to destroy the N. W. Co. fort, which stood near that of the H. B. Co.; but, meeting with unexpected resistance, they retired with the loss of one of their principal chiefs, and some others killed and wounded; since which time they have been more peaceable. They now form about 80 tents, containing 240 men bearing arms.

The Sarcees are a distinct nation, and have an entirely different language from any other of the plains; it is difficult to acquire, from the many gutteral sounds it contains. Their land was formerly on the N. side of the Saskatchewan, but they removed to the south side, and now dwell commonly S. of the Beaver Hills, near the Slaves, with whom they are at peace. They have the name of being a brave and warlike people, with whom neighboring nations always appear desirous of being upon amicable terms. Their customs and manners seem to be nearly the same as those of the Crees, and their dress is the same. Their language resembles that of the Chipewyans, many words being exactly the same; from this, and their apparent emigration from the N., we have reason to suppose them of that nation....Of late years their numbers have much augmented; in the summer of 1809, when they were all in one camp, they formed 90 tents, containing about 150 men bearing arms.

The Missourie on the S., the Rocky Mountains on the W., and the North Branch of the Saskatchewan on the N., seem to be the bounds of the foregoing numerous tribes, beyond which all are considered as enemies.

So ends Henry's 'Ethnography of Fort Vermillion.' In 1813, he went from the Saskatchewan country to Fort George (Astoria), at the mouth of the Columbia River, and May 22, 1814, he, Donald McTavish, and five *voyageurs*, were drowned when attempting to go to the Isaac Todd, anchored in the river opposite the fort. In Part III, of his 'Journals,' he had much to say about the Indian tribes west of the Rocky Mountains. His hatred of them was even more pronounced than those of the plains.

As I have previously explained, Henry's name for the Blackfeet tribes, Slave Indians, he and other early fur-traders in the Northwest got from the Ojibways and Crees. Henry's 'Painted Feather's band,' of the 'Slaves,' were the Sik'sika, the Blackfeet proper, now numbering about seven hundred and fifty, and living upon their reservation, sixty miles east of Calgary, Alberta. It is said that they so named themselves because their moccasins were generally black from their walking over the burned plains. An ancient tradition, however, gives another reason for the name: In the very long ago, an old man and his three married sons, and their women and children, were near starvation, because of the scarcity of deer and elk, so they set out to try to find a better game country. They crossed some mountains, and for the first time came to a treeless country: great plains, upon which were countless numbers of huge, dark-haired animals new to them, the buffalo. The three sons attempted to approach and kill some of them, and failed, as the animals always outran them. Then, in accordance with a vision that the old father had, he made a black-colored medicine, rubbed some of it upon his eldest son's feet, and it enabled him to run so swiftly that he easily overtook and killed some of the strange animals. Whereupon the old father said that Blackfeet should thereafter be his name. At that, the two other sons became jealous of their elder brother, and demanded that they also be given some of the black medicine. The old man refused to give it, for, he said, his vision had plainly shown him that it was to be used only by his eldest son. However, they should also have new names, and they must earn them: they should go far away upon discovery of the new country and its life, and upon their return he would name them in accordance with what they had done. The two sons departed, and were gone a long time. The younger of the two, who went south, returned with several beautifully tanned and painted buffalo robes which he had obtained from a friendly tribe that he had met, so his father named him Pikû'ni (Far-Off Robes). The other son, who went east, brought back scalps of a number of enemies that he had killed, and he was therefore named, Ah-ka-i'na (Many Chiefs). Such was the origin of the three tribes.

The Ah-ka-i´na, or as it is now shortened, the Kai´na, are the Blood Indian tribe, numbering twelve hundred, living upon their reservation, just east of Waterton Lakes National Park, Alberta, and often frequenting the Park, to the delight of the tourists who gather there every summer. They feel insulted when called Blood Indians, the whites' name for them since the time of the earliest fur-traders, Henry and others. Their Ojibway and Cree interpreters informed them that the tribe were the Mikwin´iwuk (Rey People, or Bloody People), so named because they so profusely painted their faces and robe with the native paint of the country, red ochre.

The Pikû´ni (Henry's and Cocking's Piegans) are in worse case than the Kai´na, for they are the Blackfeet of the United States Indian Bureau Their reservation adjoins Glacier National Park and they are still the largest of the three tribes numbering at present about three thousand souls.

Long before Alexander Henry's time in the Northwest, a part of the Ah´paitûpi (Blood People) gens of the Pikû´ni separated from the tribe and lived for the greater part of the time close up to the foot of the Rockies, between the St. Mary's River and the South Branch of the Saskatchewan. Henry named them the 'Cold Band; doubtless because their chief at that time was named Us′toyimstan (Cold Maker). Eventually they became the Apû′tositûpi (North People), or more properly, Apû′tosi Pikû′ni (North Pikû′ni) North Piegans of the Canadian Government. Their reservation is a short distance west of Macleod, Alberta. They number about four hundred and fifty, nearly all of them full-blood Indians.

Several Northwestern adventurers, later than Henry, mentioned still another tribe of the 'Slaves,' the Small Robes tribe. It was not a tribe, but a gens of the Pikû′ni, so numerous and so warlike that it fearlessly separated from the tribe for months at a time to camp about and hunt by itself. The gens is still existent, though its members are few.

Henry named the Missouri River as the southern boundary of the country of the Blackfeet tribes. The Yellowstone River was its southern limit. Every typographical feature, every river, creek, mountain range, and lone butte between those streams has its Blackfeet name. Favorite camping and hunting localities of the tribes, particularly the Pikû′ni, were the Prickly Pear Valley, the Three Forks of the Missouri, the Musselshell River, the bases of the Belt, the Judith, the Moccasin, and the Snowy Mountains, and the valley of the

Yellowstone in the plains. The Jefferson River Pass in the Rockies — their Ah'wotan Inahpît'si Itûk'tai (Shield Floated-Down River) — was one of their favorite routes to the country of their West-Side enemies. Equally completely named by the Blackfeet tribes are the topographical features of their one-time territory between the Missouri and the North Saskatchewan.

Henry wrote that the devices used in painting the lodges of the Blackfeet 'are taken from beasts and birds; the buffalo and the bear are frequently delineated, but in a rough and uncouth manner.' Would that he, and the fur-traders earlier than he, had been sufficiently interested to learn the reason for those pictographs! Would that they had been as much interested in the history, manners and customs, and beliefs of the tribes, as they were in the furs that they might obtain from them! For theirs was the opportunity to give light on some anthropological problems of those Northwest tribes which now can never be solved.

CHAPTER II

NITA'PIWAKSIN (REAL FOOD)

THE Blackfeet tribes had three major complexes: food, religion, and war. Until the buffalo were exterminated, and the tribes were obliged to abandon their nomadic life and retire to their several reservations, they never suffered from want of food. Îk'sîsakwi (meat) was their staff of life. They had another name for it: Nitä'piwaksîn (real food). All other foods, such as vegetables and the various grains, were kî'stäpiwaksîn (useless food). This latter term, however, did not include mi'näpi (the berry kinds), which were, in a way, sacred food.

Before the fur-traders began buying the hides of deer, elk, antelope, moose, and bighorns, the Blackfeet killed only enough of them to furnish light leather (buckskin) for their clothing and summer wraps. Nor were they, before the advent of the traders, killers of fur animals, other than a few beavers to obtain their scent glands for perfume, and otters for their beautiful fur, which was considered very sacred. They ate the meat of the deer kinds that they killed, but their mainstay, the food of which they never tired, was the meat of the buffalo. They had various ways of killing the animals: by approaching them on foot, running them on swift trained horses; and by enticing them to their *piskans* (corrals) or 'pounds,' as the early fur-traders called them. Henry wrote of the Pikû´ni (Piegans) that 'So much do these people abhor work that, to avoid the trouble of making proper pounds, they seek some precipice along the bank of the river, to which they extend their ranks and drive the buffalo headlong over it. If not killed or entirely disabled by the fall, the animals are generally so much bruised as to be easily dispatched with the bow and arrows.' But Henry was familiar with the laboriously built and none too effective *piskans* of the Assiniboins and the Crees; he could not or would not see that the cliff *piskans*, with their much deeper drop, were far more effective than those with an artificial drop of only four or five feet. And again, here was another opportunity for a detrimental remark about the people whose trade he sought. He knew, too, that the Blackfeet, at times, built *piskans*, or 'pounds,' like those of the Crees. Henry's description of one of the artificial drop *piskans* is as follows:

The pounds are of different dimentions, according to the number of tents in one camp. The common size is from 60 to 100 paces or yards in circumferance, and about five feet in height. Trees are cut down, laid upon one another, and interwoven with branches and green twigs; small openings are left to admit the dogs to feed upon the carcasses of the bulls, which are generally left as useless. This inclosure is commonly made between two hummocks, on the declivity or at the foot of rising ground. The entrance is about 10 paces wide and always faces the plains. On each side of this entrance commences a thick range of facines, the two ranges spreading asunder as they extend, to the distance of 100 yards, beyond which openings are left at intervals; but the facines soon become more thinly planted, and continue to spread apart to right and left, until each range has been extended about 300 yards from the pound. The labor is then diminished by only placing at intervals three or four cross-sticks, in imitation of a dog or other animal (sometimes called 'dead men'); these extend on the plain for about two miles, and double rows of them are planted in several other directions to a still greater distance. Young men are usually sent out to collect and bring in the buffalo — a tedious task which requires great patience, for the herd must be started by slow degrees. This is done by setting fire to dung or grass. Three young men will bring in a herd of several hundred from a great distance. When the wind is aft it is most favorable, as they can then direct the buffalo with great ease. Having come in sight of the ranges, they generally drive the herd faster, until it begins to enter the ranges, where a swift footed person has been stationed with a buffalo robe over his head, to imitate that animal; but sometimes a horse performs this business.

When he sees buffaloes approaching, he moves slowly toward the pound until they appear to him; then he sets off at full speed, imitating a buffalo as well as he can, with the herd after him. The young men in the rear now discover themselves, and drive the herd on with all possible speed. There is always a sentinel on some elevated spot to notify the camp when the buffalo appear; and this intelligence is no sooner given than every man, woman, and child runs to the ranges that lead to the pound, to prevent buffalo from taking a wrong direction. There they lie down between the facines and cross-sticks, and if the buffalo attempt to break through, the people wave their robes, which causes the herd to keep on, or turn to the opposite side, where other persons do the same. When the buffalo have been thus directed to the entrance of the pound, the Indian who leads rushes into it and out the other side, either by jumping over the enclosure or creeping through an opening left for that purpose. The buffalo tumble in pell-mell at his heels, almost exhausted, but keep moving around the enclosure from E. to W., and never in a direction against the sun. What appeared extraordinary to me, on those occasions, was that, when word was given to the camp of the near approach of the buffalo, the dogs would skulk away from the pound, and not approach it until the herd entered. Many buffaloes break their legs, and some their necks, jumping into the pound, as the descent is generally six or eight feet and stumps are left standing there. The buffalo being caught, the men assemble at the inclosure, armed with bows and arrows; every arrow has a particular mark of its owner, and they fly until the whole herd is killed. Then the men enter the compound, and each claims his own; but commonly there is what they term the master of the pound, who divides the animals and gives each tent an equal share, reserving nothing for himself. But in the end he is always the best provided for, as it is in his tent that the numerous ceremonies relating to the pound are observed.

It was an Assiniboin *piskan* that Henry thus described. In 1776, his uncle, Alexander Henry, in describing an Assiniboin *piskan*, wrote as follows:

At daylight, several of the more expert hunters were sent to decoy the animals into the pound. They were dressed in Ox-skins [buffalo robes] with the hair and horns. Their faces were covered, and their gestures so closely resembled those of the animals themselves, that, had I not been in the secret, I should have been as much deceived as the oxen.

At ten o'clock, one of the hunters returned, bringing information of the herd. Immediately all the dogs were muzzled; and this done, the whole crowd of men and women surrounded the outside of the pound.

The herd, of which the extent was so great that I cannot pretend to estimate its numbers, was distant half a mile, advancing slowly, and frequently stopping to feed. The part, played by the decoyers, was that of approaching them within hearing, and then bellowing like themselves. On hearing the noise, the oxen did not fail to give it their attention; and, whether from curiosity or sympathy, advanced to meet those from whom it proceeded. These, in the meantime, fell back deliberately toward the pound, always repeating the call, whenever the oxen stopped. This was reiterated till the leaders of the herd had followed the decoyers into the jaws of the pound, which, though wide asunder toward the plain, terminated, like a funnel, in a small aparture, or gateway; and, within this was the pound itself. The Indians remark, that in all herds of animals there are chiefs, or leaders, by whom the motions of all the rest are determined.

The decoyers now retired within the pound, and were followed by the oxen. But, the former retired still further, withdrawing themselves at certain movable parts of the fence, while the latter were fallen upon by all the hunters, and presently wounded, and killed, by showers of arrows.

Amid the uproar which ensued, the oxen made several attempts to force the fence; but the Indians stopped them, and drove them back, by shaking skins before their eyes. Skins were also made use of to stop the entrance, being let down by strings, as soon as the oxen were inside. The slaughter was prolonged till the evening, when the hunters retired to their tents. Next morning, all the tongues were presented to the chief, to number of seventy-two.[1]

All the old-time buffalo hunters, Indians and whites, agree with me that Alexander Henry, the younger, was wrong when he stated that 'Young men are sent out to collect and bring in the buffalo — a tedious task which requires great patience, for the herd must be started by slow degrees. This is done by setting fire to dung or grass.'

While buffalo herds were quite easily decoyed by arousing their curiosity, we cannot believe that they were ever made to move in a desired direction by being driven. Inevitably they would have become frightened and have gone off on the run, and always with heads to the wind; for their power of scent was stronger than their sight in detecting the presence of their great enemy, man. My old friend Eli Guardipe, or Ai´isînamakan (Takes-Gun-First), for many years a member of the Pikû´ni tribe of the Blackfeet, lived with the Crees, Assiniboins, and French mixed bloods of those tribes in his boyhood days. He tells me that during that time, in the Turtle Mountain

[1] *Travels and adventures in Canada and the Indian Territories Between the Years 1760 and 1776.* By Alexander Henry. Edited by James Bain. Boston, Little, Brown & Company, 1901.

country of North Dakota north of it, he saw several herds of buffalo decoyed to positions where the concealed hunters could easily dash in among them, upon their trained buffalo horses, and make great killings. The decoying was always done by men on horseback and covered with buffalo robes, who, approaching a herd as near as they dared, began bellowing and retreating, going out of sight whenever possible, and reappearing, and disappearing, and in that way so exciting their inquisitiveness that they eventually had the herd following them on a swift run. There can be no doubting my old friend's testimony as to this, for he is an absolutely truthful man.

I have given 'corral,' as the translation of the Blackfeet *piskan*. It is not that; for some days, Guardipe, Many Tail Feathers, and I have been discussing the real meaning of the word, and we have decided that the nearest we can come to it, in English, is 'remaining place.'

The Blackfeet tribes had *piskans* in all parts of their country, from the Saskatchewan south to the Yellowstone, and they were all of like character: the fall was a cliff, at the foot of which was a stout, half-circle corral, made of tree-trunks and branches and rocks. Directly above the corral was the apex of the great V of rock-piles which extended out upon the plain for several miles, the outer ends of the two lines about a half-mile to three fourths of a mile apart.

The *ahwawakiks* (callers-in), of whom there were several in each tribe of the Blackfeet, were looked upon as very sacred men, to whom Sun had given power to entice the buffalo into the great V of rock-piles, so that the people concealed at the piles could frighten and drive them on to the cliff edge and to quick death in the corral at its base. The callers-in or decoyers of the buffalo always disguised themselves with buffalo robes and buffalo head masks, and went out to bring in a herd either on foot or on horseback. This could not be accomplished, however, and was never attempted, when the wind was from the *piskan* toward the herd.

A *piskan* that can be easily visited by Glacier National Park tourists is at a cliff on the north side of the Two Medicine (Lodges) River, about a mile above Holy Family Mission, and a mile below the Park-to-Park Highway. Where the corral or holding place stood are from three to five feet of decomposed remains of buffalo, and, strange to say, great quantities of maggot shells, which endure long after the bones and horns of the animals upon which the flies fed and deposited their eggs have turned into dust. Arrow-heads and other flint implements are plentiful in and around this ancient *piskan*.

The very last *piskan* which the Pikû´ni tribe of the Blackfeet used was one that they had several miles above the present town of Chouteau, Teton County. On a day in the 1850s, as near as we can determine it, a very large herd of buffalo was successfully decoyed there, a brown river of the animals falling from the cliff edge down into the *piskan*. That night, a man of the tribe, Many Tail Feathers, had a vision, as the Blackfeet call a dream.

A buffalo bull came to him and said: 'My son, you are doing my children great wrong: you Pikû´ni are killing so many of them that they are fast decreasing in number, and, unless you cease decoying them into your *piskan*, they must soon all perish. Now, this I ask of you: destroy your *piskan* that you have here, and cease using your other ones. If you will do so, I will give you some of my sacred power, my medicine. It is so very powerful that it will keep you safe from the bullets and the arrows of your enemies. So shall you become a great warrior and a chief of your people. Now, then, your answer.'

'I shall do as you request. I will destroy this *piskan*, and urge my people to cease using our others,' Many Tail Feathers replied.

The buffalo bulls' chief then told him just what articles he should procure and keep, as the insignia of the buffalo bull chief medicine, and taught him, also, the songs of the medicine. The bull chief then vanished.

Many Tail Feathers awoke, and was almost overcome when he realized what a very powerful vision it was that he had experienced. Soon after daylight, he went out and set fire to the fence of the *piskan*, and, returning to camp, told the people that he had burned it, and for what reason. Later on, the chiefs of the tribe invited him to their council, and, having heard him relate his vision, they decided that the buffalo bull chief was right about the *piskans*, for by decoying herds of buffalo to them, it often happened that many more of the animals were killed than the people could use; they therefore ordered that, from that day, the *piskans* should remain forever idle. And as the buffalo bull chief promised Many Tail Feathers, so did he prosper. He had many battles with the enemies of the Pikû´ni, killed many of them, and always came out of a fight without so much as a scratch upon his body.

Because of his bravery and his kindness and generosity to all of his people who needed help, he became a very great chief and lived to extreme old age.

Such is the reason the Pikû'ni give for abandonment of the *piskan* as a means of procuring meat. The real reason, however, was that, with its own steamboat transportation on the Missouri River, the American Fur Company, at its Fort Union and Fort Benton posts, would buy all the buffalo robes that the Blackfeet tribes could tan. That meant the end of community (*piskan*) killings of the animals. Each man of them now was eager to hunt for himself and his family; the more robes that his women could tan, the richer he would be in the coveted useful and ornamental goods of the white men. Incidentally, this was a severe blow to the Hudson's Bay Company. Transportation was so difficult and expensive between its Saskatchewan posts and deep water, at York Factory, Hudson's Bay, that it could not afford to buy bulky buffalo robes, a few bales of which would fill a large canoe or batteau. Therefore, it lost the trade for beaver and other fur skins that it had had with the Blackfeet and their allies, the Gros Ventres and Saksi.

In the buffalo days, the Blackfeet and their allies, and other plains tribes as well, always had a supply of dried foods for times when fresh meat was not to be had. The main one of these foods was dried meat. The hams, loins, and parts of the fore shoulders of buffalo, and even of deer and elk, were cut into sheet pieces of various sizes, about a half-inch thick, and dried in the sun, or, in case of bad weather, upon lines strung from pole to pole above the lodge fires. When perfectly dry, the sheets were brittle and could be eaten as they were, or boiled, or broiled before the fire. Dried back fat of the buffalo was generally eaten with the dried meat, much as we eat butter with bread.

Another dried food was pemmican. This was made by roasting sheets of dried meat, and then finely desiccating them upon a flat rock with a small rock for a hammer. The meat was then mixed with marrow grease, obtained by boiling the broken-up leg bones of buffalo or deer, and sometimes dried service berries or dried and pounded choke cherries were added to the mass, along with a few leaves of mint. The pemmican was then tightly packed in sacks made of the fresh raw hide of buffalo, deer, or elk; the ends of the sacks were tightly closed by sewing with sinew thread. Pemmican so made and sacked would remain in perfect condition for many months. It was very nutritious and sustaining food. 'Pemmican' is a Cree word, accented on the last syllable, and means, as we have it in English, a mixture. Moka′ki, the Blackfeet word for it, means, gathered food.

Other dried foods of the Blackfeet were cherries, bull berries, service berries, blueberries, and wild turnips. The cherries were finely pounded, stones and all, before drying.

Although camas, a bulbous species of the lily family, is as plentiful upon the east slope of the Rockies as it is on the west slope, the Blackfeet women did not gather and roast quantities of it for winter use, as did the women of the Kû′tenai, Kal′ispel, Spokan′, and other West-Side tribes. The roasting of the bulbs required just the right amount of heat. A pit was dug in the ground, lined with small stones, and a fire built upon them. When the stones became red-hot, they and the coals of the fire were covered with a thin layer of earth. On top of that was placed a layer of green grass; then a layer of the camas; another layer of grass; more camas; and so on until the pit was filled. Then, upon top of still another layer of earth, a fire was built and kept burning for three days and three nights, after which the roasted bulbs were taken from the pit and stored in the lodges of the roasters. They were very sticky and sweet, nutritious food.

It was a belief of the Blackfeet that, if a pit of camas proved to be improperly roasted, over-cooked or undercooked, death would soon come to the roasters or to their relatives. For that reason they did not gather and roast it. But when at peace with the West-Side tribes, as sometimes happened, they eagerly traded buffalo robes and buffalo leather for all of it that they could possibly obtain.

The *pièce de resistance* of the Blackfeet, a dish that would delight any epicure, was — and is — säpot´sîsts: stuffed entrail, prepared as follows: the small intestine of a buffalo, elk, deer, or other ruminant, which is streaked with white fat, is thoroughly washed, and then stuffed with small pieces of loin, the tenderest meat of the animal, the intestine being turned inside out during the stuffing process, and so bringing the white fat streaks in connection with the stuffing. The ends of the intestine are then tied and broiled on live coals of a fire, it being constantly turned and moved about until sufficiently cooked, when it is thrust into a kettle of boiling water for a few moments, and then is ready to serve. By this process all the delicate juices and flavors of the meat are preserved. Six inches of the stuffed intestine is a liberal portion. A fortune could be made by any first-class restaurateur, in any city, who would make a specialty of this Blackfeet dish.

Unlike the Sioux, Crees, Crows, and other neighboring tribes, the Blackfeet never ate dogs. Nor, until after the extermination of the buffalo, did they ever eat fish or water animals, and water fowl, as these are believed to be the property of the dread Suyi Tupi (Water People), human beings who live in the depths of the rivers and lakes, and drown and draw down to their under-water lodges the people of the earth, at every opportunity.

Buffalo, elk, deer, antelope, bighorn, and moose were so plentiful in the country of the Blackfeet tribes, that their killings of them made no impression upon their numbers until long after the English and American fur-traders began buying buffalo robes and the hides of the other animals. It is more than probable that more buffalo were annually drowned in the rivers of the country than were killed by the various tribes of the plains. The following is Henry's description of drowned buffalo that he saw:

March 30, 1801. Rain broke up the ice; it drifted in large masses, malting a great noise by crushing,' tumbling, and tossing in every direction, driven by a strong current. It continued to drift on the 31st, bearing great numbers of buffalo from above, which must have been drowned in attempting to cross while the ice was weak....

Wednesday, April 1. The river clear of ice, but drowned buffalo continue to drift by in entire herds....It is really astonishing what vast numbers have perished; they formed one continuous line in the current for two days and nights. One of my men found a herd that had fallen through the ice in Park River and all had been drowned....

April 18. Rain. Drowned buffalo still drifting down the river, but not in such vast numbers as before, many having lodged on the banks and along the beach.

April 25. Drowned buffalo drift down the river day and night.

May 1. The stench from the vast numbers of drowned buffalo along the river was intolerable.... They tell me that the number of buffalo lying along the beach and on the banks above passes all imagination; they form one continuous line and emit a horrid stench. I am informed that every spring it is about the same.

In corroboration of Henry's account is this from the John McDonnell Journal, under date of May 18, 1795, when descending the Qu'Appelle River.

Observing a good many carcasses of buffaloes in the river and along its banks, I was taken up the whole day with counting them, and, to my surprise, I found I had numbered when we put up at night, 7,360, drowned and mired along the river and in it. It is true, in one or two places, I went on shore and walked from one carcass to the other, where they lay from three to five files deep.[1]

---

[1]Masson, vol. I, 1889, page 294.

As late as the spring of 1880, at our trading-post on the Missouri River, thirty miles above the mouth of the Musselshell River, I myself saw some hundreds of drowned buffalo drifting down-stream after the ice went out. And in the summer time, I have often seen buffalo mired down, dead, and dying, in the quicksands of the Upper Missouri, generally under cutbanks of the river. Having decided to cross a river, a herd of buffalo plunged into it without regard for a landing-place on the other side. So was it that the animals found themselves, oftentimes, facing a cut-bank instead of a sloping shore, and usually, under the cutbanks, if the water was shallow, the mud was so tenacious that it caught and held the animals and they slowly sank deeper in it until, after many hours, they were either drowned or died from want of food. I cannot remember that I ever saw any elk, deer, or antelope in like predicament, although these animals swam from one side to another of the river even more frequently than did the buffalo.

So far as I can learn, there was no north-to-south and south-to-north migration of the buffalo herds in the Yellowstone, Missouri, Saskatchewan country, as there was said to have been in the plains country crossed by the Overland Trail. Yet Blackfeet tradition has it that there were times when the buffalo suddenly left certain sections of their country, and the people were reduced to the starvation point before they found the herds again. Of such a time is the legend in the following chapter.

CHAPTER III

WHEN MEN AND ANIMALS WERE FRIENDLY

IN the early part of a very long-ago winter, the Pikû´ni were encamped south of Elk River (Red Deer River, Alberta) and killing buffalo as they needed them. But one morning, when they arose and went outside their lodges, they could not see any of the animals, not even a single old bull. Where, at sunset, herds of them had grazed, there was now naught but lifeless plain; not even an antelope upon it. But this did not cause the people to worry; all were confident that the herds would soon return; so the hunters rested in their lodges, smoking, gambling, dancing, telling stories, and eating of the dried meat and pemmican, back fat, and berry soup that their women set before them. Days and nights passed; the plain remained barren of the buffalo and antelope, the dry food supply of the people diminished, and, when starvation faced them, they broke camp and went in search of the vanished herds; all but one man, who said that he would remain right where he was, for he was certain that the buffalo would soon return.

This man, White Eagle, had two wives and son of about ten winters. When the dried food in his lodge was gone, he had them go out and gather berries; and when the few that they could find had been eaten, they began to starve.

To the north of this starving family, at Shell Butte, on Elk River, were encamped all the various kinds of meat-eating animals, each kind in a group by itself; the lodges in the particular part of the camp circle which belonged to each kind. In that long-ago time, it must be remembered, the various kinds of animals had the power — given to them by Sun himself — to change themselves into human beings, and back into their right selves, whenever they chose to do so.

Each kind of animals in this great camp circle had its chief, and the greatest of them all was Chief Spotted Wolf. After him in importance was Big Wolf; then in the following order came Black Wolf, Mountain Lion, and Lynx. These were the head chiefs. The lesser chiefs were: Coyote, Wolverine, Red Fox, Black Fox, Badger, Skunk.

Spotted Wolf's son, wandering about upon the plain one evening, discovered the lodge of the starving people; by the red glow of the fire within it, he knew that it was occupied. He cautiously, silently went up to it, looked in, and was surprised when he saw that the occupants were human beings and apparently dying from want of food. He felt great pity for them, and at once turned homeward, arriving in camp just as day was breaking; and when he told his father what he had discovered, he, too, at once felt pity for the starving people. He called a council of the chiefs about it, and they decided that the poor human beings should be helped. They ordered the sons of Big Wolf, Coyote, Red Fox, and Black Fox to go to their aid, as they were all four of them very swift of feet. They departed, carrying food for the starving ones.

That evening, White Eagle and his family heard the crunching of snow; footsteps of persons approaching their lodge; and then the stamping of feet just outside the doorway.

'Come in, come in,' White Eagle feebly called out, and entered, one by one, four strangers, each with a pouch of food, which he at once laid upon the women's side of the lodge. White Eagle told them that they were welcome in his poor lodge. He gave them seats upon the guest side of the lodge, noticing their dress as they took their places. Each one wore a robe of the animal which he really was, and a headdress, too, and all had necklaces of shells. It was noticed that their faces were rather long and narrow. Wolf was their spokesman. He told White Eagle that, learning of the trouble he was in, the chief of his camp had sent him and his companions to aid him. There in the pouches was food: dried entrails, dried back fat. He advised that the starving ones should eat sparingly at first. The camp of his people was at Shell Butte, and the head chief, named Spotted Wolf, wanted the starving ones to move up there, where they would have plenty to eat.

The starving ones ate but a little of the food so strangely brought to them, and were not troubled in their insides. They did not know what to think of their four visitors; they had never seen the like of them. White Eagle wanted to ask who they were, of what tribe, but was afraid to question them.

The next morning Big Wolf's son said to White Eagle: 'We brought you but a little food, not sufficient for our need while traveling, so this morning we four will go out and make a killing in a herd of buffalo that we saw, yesterday, not far from here.'

'Ha! The buffalo have returned, then! I thought that they would. I am glad. I will go with you,' said White Eagle.

'No. You are weak from long starvation. You remain here in your lodge. We will soon return with plenty of meat, you and your family will eat plenty of it, and so be strong enough to start for our camp in the morning,' Big Wolf replied.

The four took up their weapons and went off northward, and a little later, White Eagle followed their trail, to learn what he could of them. He saw them in the distance, walking along in single file, and suddenly they disappeared; vanished, right in the open plain. Then appeared a small herd of buffalo, swiftly running, and he saw four animals in pursuit, the leader a wolf, next a coyote, then a black fox, and last a red fox. He saw the wolf cut a small buffalo from the herd, seize it by its head, and bring it to the ground, and at that all four of the animals tore into its throat and soon killed it.

Greatly troubled, White Eagle hurried home and told his women what he had seen. They replied that he must have been mistaken. There was no mistake about it; his eyes did not lie, he said. Actually, the four had suddenly changed into animals, and in pursuing the buffalo they had ran with their tails stiffly up, each in the line according to his fleetness, wolf first, coyote next, black fox third, and red fox last. At that, his women believed he was telling the truth. They were terribly worried; so was he; they knew not what to do. Said one of the women: 'My man, the things that the four wear are proof that they are really animals. Each of them has a robe and a headdress, representative of his own kind. Yes, and even each one's face has a certain resemblance to the face of the animal that he really is. Oh, what shall we do? What shall we do?'

'They are four, and I am but one, and weak. We must do as they say. They have fed us; they are after more meat for us; it may be that they intend to do us not harm, but good,' White Eagle replied.

Came in Black Fox and Red Fox with some fat meat; then Wolf and Coyote with more meat, and all ate heartily, each broiling pieces of it before the fire. The women then cut the remainder of the meat into thin strips and hung the pieces above the fire to dry. All was going well, so White Eagle and his women and his son lost most of their fear of the strange guests.

On the following morning, they broke camp and moved northward. The animal-men went well ahead, and when the others overtook them, near night, there was the snow cleared away where the lodge was to stand, and the ice in the river had been broken, so that the women could easily get water. This kindness on the part of the animal-men lessened White Eagle's and his women's fear of them. In the evening, after all had finished eating, Big Wolf said that he and his companions would go on to their camp, which was now not far away, and that he himself would return in the morning to guide White Eagle to it. They all arose and left the lodge, and one of the women, quickly looking out through a slit in the door curtain, gave a little cry of fear, and, turning back to her couch, said that she had seen them going off in their other, their animal shapes, tails stiffly up and running swiftly.

Fear again came upon the four in the little lodge. What was the end of this to be, this intercourse they were having with animal-men? Were. they, perhaps, being decoyed on to some terrible fate?

The four young animal-men returned to their camp and told Big Wolf and the other chiefs that they had taken the food to the human beings just in time to save them from starving to death, and that they now had the lodge of them near by, and would bring them to the big camp circle the following day.

The lesser chiefs left to Big Wolf just what should be done in the way of receiving the human beings and entertaining them. In the morning, when his son left to guide them in to camp, he ordered all the animals to turn into human beings and set up their lodges, and told his wives to clear the snow from the place where the strangers would put up their lodge. Furthermore, he ordered that all should remain in their lodges when the humans arrived, so that they would not be embarrassed by being stared at. He knew that his animal kinds would be eager to see the arrivals, for very few of them, up to this time, had ever seen real human beings.

It was midday when Big Wolf's son brought White Eagle and his family to the great camp of the animals. They saw that the lodges were, the most of them, large and well made, but thought it strange that the occupants were all of them inside; not even a single child was in sight. Their guide led them to the cleared space where they were to set up their lodge, and his wife came out and helped them set it. When that was done, their guide said to White Eagle: 'My father, Big Wolf, invites you to his lodge, so come with me.'

This lodge of Big Wolf, head chief of the camp, was a very large one. Just above the doorway was a finely tanned wolfskin, decorated with feathers of bright colors. As they were about to enter the lodge, they heard Big Wolf singing a beautiful, a powerful song, one beginning with the words, 'My lodge is sacred.' He ceased singing it, and ordered his woman to set fire to some incense; and as the sweet-scented smoke arose, he called out to White Eagle, 'Enter, my friend.' And then, motioning him to a seat on his right: 'I welcome you. My friend, this, my lodge, I give to you, and also my songs, my sacred songs.'

White Eagle remained in the lodge for some time, learning the sacred songs, and talking with his host about various things, and as he was about to leave, his host said to him: 'The chief of each band of us here will in turn invite you to his lodge. I advise you to accept all the invitations except two. When the chief of the skunks invites you, do not go to his lodge, for you know what they are, what a fearful odor they emit. The badgers are nearly as odorous as the skunks, so, when the badger chief invites you, as he surely will, be you deaf to his call, as you were when Chief Skunk shouted his invitation. Another thing: do not you, your women nor your son, pick up any property that you may see lying about in camp, else there will be trouble. Be sure to tell your family this, as soon as you get home.'

White Eagle did that. He and his women wondered just what Big Wolf meant by the warning; what would happen if they did take something in the camp. But they decided to take no chances; no matter what they might see lying about, no matter how valuable it might be, they would not even touch it.

On the following morning, the chief of the Big Long-Tails (cougar, mountain lion) had his women dress in their best, take food to White Eagle and his family, with an invitation for him to visit the chief. These women had their faces painted yellow, that being the sacred color paint of the Big Long-Tails.

White Eagle found that the lodge of this chief was painted yellow. Above the doorway was a tanned big long-tail skin, beautifully tanned, and decorated with bright-colored feathers. The chief welcomed him, feasted him, and talked with him about various things, and then, as Big Wolf had done, advised him that he should avoid a certain black greasy lodge in the camp circle, and a squatty poor lodge next to it. The one, the lodge of Chief Skunk, the other, the squatty one, Chief Badger's lodge. Both these chiefs were unpleasant to meet, because of the bad odor that they constantly emitted.

On the next day, White Eagle was called

to the lodge of Black Wolf, and found him a very handsome, dark-faced man. And again he was advised to keep away from Chief Skunk and Chief Badger. He began to feel sorry for the two; they seemed to have no friends in the big camp.

Next to invite White Eagle was Little Long-Tail (lynx). He was of rather poor appearance; his lodge and his women were just ordinary. But, like the other chiefs, he gave White Eagle his lodge, and taught him the sacred songs that went with it. Also, even more strongly than the others, he advised him to keep away from Chief Skunk and Chief Badger.

The chief of the coyotes was next to invite the man to sit and feast with him. He was a very handsome man; had a fine lodge; fine women. He, too, advised White Eagle to be deaf to any invitation from Chief Skunk and Chief Badger to visit in their lodges.

On this day, Big Wolf came out of his lodge and made an explanation to the camp: 'The reason I am having you all invite this human being to visit you in your lodges is, that he and his women are not our kind, and I want you to become well acquainted with him.'

Red Fox, and then Black Fox, feasted White Eagle, gave him their lodges, and their sacred songs. After he had visited them, Chief Kit Fox invited him. These last were very slender people, with thin, sharp faces. This chief also advised the man to keep away from the black greasy lodge and the squatty lodge, in which lived the bad odored Skunk Chief, and the Badger Chief.

White Eagle had now visited all the chiefs of the camp, except Skunk and Badger. Big Wolf had invited Chief Wolverine and his people to join the camp, but, for some unknown reason, he refused to come near it. He remained at some distance up the river, where there was a buffalo fall.

On the morning after White Eagle visited Kit Fox, Chief Skunk came out of his lodge, and, in a clear, loud voice, invited the man to come and sit and feast with him.

Said White Eagle to his women: 'There! That is the invitation I have been dreading to hear. You know that we have been advised to have nothing to do with him. Well, I will not go to his lodge.'

Just then all the people of the great camp turned back into the kinds of animals which they really were. Several of them snapped at, actually bit White Eagle's son, and then they all ran off; all but Chief Skunk, who stood stiffly in front of his lodge, tail straight up. The boy came running and crying to his father.

'What have you done? Have you taken something that does not belong to you?' White Eagle demanded.

Crying, terribly frightened, the boy brought out an arrow from under his robe. A beautifully straight, flint-tipped arrow, with eagle feathers tied to it. He held it to his breast and it immediately turned into dung.

'There! That was the cause of the trouble here,' said White Eagle. He remembered what Big Wolf had told him should be done in case this rule should be broken: 'Quick! Throw upon the fire the dried buffalo paunch and the dried buffalo entrails that Big Wolf's women brought to us,' he shouted to his women. They did that, and at once all the various kinds of animals turned back into the forms of human beings and returned to their lodges. And at that, White Eagle went to Big Wolf and said that he was sorry that his son had caused so much trouble.

'Don't let it happen again,' Big Wolf replied.

On the following day, the Badger Chief stepped from his lodge and shouted invitation to White Eagle to sit and feast with him.

'There! Another call that I have been dreading to hear,' White Eagle muttered.

'You had better heed it; you had better go,'

his women urged.

'Of course you would say that. You women, you are always getting men into trouble,' he replied.

Again Badger Chief shouted the invitation. White Eagle squirmed about upon his couch; shook his head. The women stared at him.

Then a third time Badger Chief shouted to him to come to his lodge. He let out a big sigh, did White Eagle; then clapped his hands together; twisted about in his seat.

'You had better go,' his oldest woman told him.

'Yes, go!' his other one advised.

He arose, wrapped his robe about him, and went across the big camp circle to Badger Chief's lodge. Chief Skunk, peeking out from his lodge, saw him entering it; said to himself: 'There goes the human being into Badger's lodge. He did not pay any attention to the call I gave him. Well, to-morrow I will again invite him over.'

Said Badger Chief to White Eagle, as he entered the lodge: 'It is well for you that you came at my third call. If I had been obliged to call you a fourth time — well, I will only say that it is all right now.'

In that far-back time, wild turnips were used for incense, as well as the better-odored sweetgrass. Badger Chief held up some dried and powdered turnip, put it upon some coals and sang:

'The earth is sacred.
My lodge is sacred.
We, the Badgers, are
The most powerful
Of all the animals.'

And then he told White Eagle that he gave him his lodge and the sacred songs that belonged to it.

That is why the skin of a badger, as well as the skins of the other kinds of animals that were in that great camp circle, is always used in the ceremonies connected with the building of the great lodge that we give to Sun, every summer.

Lastly, as White Eagle was about to return to his lodge, Badger Chief said to him: 'The one next to me, he of the black greasy lodge, he has a very bad odor; don't go near him.'

Upon his way home, White Eagle dropped into the lodge of Big Wolf, told him where he had been, and said that he believed Badger Chief to be very powerful.

'You are right. He is not tall and swift as the rest of us are, but actually he is the most powerful of us all,' Big Wolf replied.

White Eagle and his women now noticed that

the various bands of the big camp were becoming very restless, very active, the young people particularly. They went here and there in large crowds; they had exciting times all through the long nights. Big Wolf gave the reason for it: this was the mating, the breeding season.

Early the next morning, Chief Skunk put on his best clothing, set his skunkskin cap upon his head, went outside his lodge, and shouted invitation to White Eagle to come and feast with him.

'Hear him, that invitation shouter. Who is he?' White Eagle said to his women.

One of them went outside, quickly returned, and said: 'He is the chief of the Skunks. All dressed up, standing there in front of his lodge; looking this way; expecting you to go to him.'

'I cannot go to his lodge; the chiefs of all the other bands have advised me to keep away from Chief Skunk,' White Eagle replied.

Soon they heard Chief Skunk again shout the invitation; and then again; and, finally a fourth time, which, of course, would be the last time.

One of the women peeked out at him. 'He is still standing out there, looking this way,' she reported.

'Ha! He bows his head; his body bends

over; he is turning around; going slowly into his lodge; his heart is low,' she concluded.

'I can't help it; they all told me to keep away from him. I must do as they say,' White Eagle replied.

Soon after this, camp was moved down-river to fresh hunting ground.

There, later on, Big Wolf said to White Eagle: 'You see that the women of our great camp are getting big with the young within them. Well, we are all going to separate, scatter out widely, so that the women may bring forth their young in quietness and safety. So is it that you and yours must return to your people. Prepare to start to-morrow. I am going to send my son, and Chief Coyote's son, and Black Fox's son, to guide you to your people, and keep you supplied with meat until you meet them. Forget not all that we have done for you: given you our various powerful lodges, taught you the songs that go with them. You, in turn, give the lodges, the songs, to leading members of your people, all but one of them, which you will keep for yourself.'

'You have been very good to us; very generous. As you have said, so will I do,' White Eagle replied.

The great camp was broken on the following morning. White Eagle's guides, Big Wolf's son, the sons of Chief Coyote and Chief Black Fox, led off to the south, and he and his family followed. As they topped the rim of the valley and looked back down into it, they saw that all the bands of the great camp had changed into the animals that they really were, and were hurrying off in all directions to seek dens in which the females could bring forth their young. It was a wonderful sight.

White Eagle's guides kept well in the lead. Each day they killed a buffalo or other meat animal for the party. On the fourth day of their southward journey, they sighted a camp of many lodges, and Big Wolf went on ahead to investigate it. He brought back a pair of moccasins which he found near the camp, and White Eagle knew, as soon as he saw them, that they were moccasins of his own tribe. Whereupon Big Wolf said to him: 'You and yours go on and set up your lodge in the camp, and we will wait here until sundown, when, after you have burned some incense, we will join you. Do not tell your kind that we are really animals, and for this night have no visitors in your lodge.'

The family moved on into the camp and set up their lodge. The people were surprised to see them, as they believed that they were long since dead from want of food, or else had been killed by members of some enemy tribe.

Soon after Sun went down, White Eagle shouted out, so loudly that all in camp could hear him: 'My people, this I ask of you: Do not visit me to-night, as I have something to do that is very difficult.'

Soon after he made this request, a wolf howled near the camp, and the dogs howled and howled in answer. At that, White Eagle put some sweetgrass upon some coals that he drew from the lodge fire, and, as the scented smoke arose, the wolf howled again. But this time the dogs of the camp did not answer; they remained quiet, every one of them.

Soon a coyote was heard, yelping and yelping near camp. All the dogs yelped in answer. White Eagle burned more sweetgrass. Again the coyote yelped, and not a dog of the camp made answer.

Next, and last, a near-by fox gave his hoarse and cough-like bark, and all the camp dogs barked in answer to it. Again White Eagle burned sweetgrass, again the fox barked, and the camp dogs did not even whine; they remained silent, listening, every one of them. And the people, listening, too, wondered what all this meant, and were uneasy. And soon word was passed from lodge to lodge that three beautifully clothed men, strangers, had been seen entering White Eagle's lodge.

On the following morning, visitors were made welcome in White Eagle's lodge. They met there three beautifully clothed young men who were, White Eagle told them, his close friends: Big Wolf, Coyote, and Black Fox, with whom, and their three tribes, he had wintered. The visitors liked them, invited them to their lodges, became very friendly with them.

Now came summer. Camp was moved to fresh game country, and a number of the men prepared to go to war. Hearing of it, Big Wolf had them gather in White Eagle's lodge, and told them that he and his two friends would go with them against the enemy. And, to make sure that they would be successful, he taught them the wolf songs, they all sitting there in the lodge, and with sticks beating the couch rails in time to the songs, the first time that had ever been done. And from that far-back time, all war parties have sung those songs in that way, those powerful songs of the wolf, with sticks beating time to them.

Having learned the songs, the war party set out, accompanied by the three strangers. Days passed without news of the party. Then came back the three, Big Wolf, Coyote, and Black Fox, and reported that the party had fought a party of Crows, killed many of them, and would arrive home on a certain day. They did not say that they had turned back into their real selves, in order quickly to bring the good news, but White Eagle and his family knew it, and kept it to themselves. The war party did return on the day named, bringing many scalps and many belongings of the enemy, and the people rejoiced.

And now Coyote and Black Fox became anxious to return to their people, and urged Big Wolf that they depart at once. After long silence, long thinking, Big Wolf replied: 'Go, you two. Tell my people that I shall not return to them. For, as I see it, this is my duty: to remain here with this human being, White Eagle, whom I regard as my father. He is old; he needs me; I shall remain with him, and keep him and his always supplied with food.'

So was it that Coyote and Black Fox returned to their people. Big Wolf remained with White Eagle and his people. He married a fine woman; had children by her. He lived to great age.

There! So was it that our people first had intercourse with the four-footed kinds. After that, they had experiences with other animals, buffalo, beavers, and still others, which also had the power to change themselves into the forms of human beings and speak the language of human beings. They have been very helpful to us; they have given us of their sacred power.

CHAPTER IV

RELIGION

IT is more than likely that, until the Blackfeet tribes began to obtain horses, and in quest of them came in contact — sometimes peacefully — with more southern tribes, their religion differed but little from that of other Algonquins, particularly their near neighbors, the Crees, whose supreme god, or creator, was — and still is — a mythical being named Old Man. The Blackfeet tribes to-day believe that Napi (Old Man) created the earth, and all things and life upon it, but they no longer pray to him. According to their very many tales of him, he was mostly occupied in playing mischievous and mean tricks upon the various animals, and men, too.

The Blackfeet tribes are, and for a very long time have been, sun worshipers, as are the Crows, Sioux, Arapahos, Gros Ventres, and other tribes. They were in alliance with the Gros Ventres when visited by Anthony Hendry, in 1754, and probably for a long time before that, and through them were on friendly terms with the Arapahos, a branch of the Gros Ventres tribe then roaming the plains south of the Crow country, in what is now the State of Wyoming. The Arapahos were on friendly terms with tribes still farther south, who were sun worshipers, and it is likely through them they became imbued with it, and passed the belief on to the Blackfeet, and their brother tribe, the Gros Ventres. And again, it is possible that members of the Blackfeet tribes, roaming far south in quest of horses, themselves met some of the pueblo tribes, and, remaining with them for some time, in that way became sun worshipers. Certain it is that the Blackfeet acquired from more southern tribes the belief that the sun is the supreme god of the universe, and in the course of time, and little by little, themselves created some of the very elaborate and spectacular rites and ceremonials with which they worship it. But they believe that it was one of their own far-back ancestors, Scar-Face, who gave them their knowledge of the sun and taught them to worship it. Briefly, the legend is as follows:

I

THE SCAR-FACE MYTH

In that far-back time, a very poor young man, who had upon his face a deep scar, asked a very beautiful young girl to marry him. She laughed at him, made fun of him, and replied that, when he removed the scar from his face, she would do as he asked.

Scar-Face left camp; wandered far in quest of some way to remove his disfigurement. He met, one after another, many animals, and asked them to help him, but always they referred him to some other animal, farther on, who, they said, might have the power to efface the scar. So traveling, he came at last to the shore of a great lake; so large was it that, if there was land on its other side, he could not see it. He had now met all the animals, obtained no help from them, and so, discouraged, lay down at the edge of the water to die. Came then two swans swimming near the shore, and asked him what was his trouble. He told them, and they said that far out in the lake was an island on which Sun had his home, and they believed that he could remove the scar. Anyhow, they would take him to the island, and he could ask Sun to do it.

As the swans told him to do, he lay down upon their backs and they bore him out to the island. He landed, and at once met a handsome young man who told him that he was Early Riser (Morning Star); that Sun was his father, and

Night-Light (the moon) his mother. His father was away upon his daily journey across the blue, but his mother was at home; he would take Scar-Face to her and she would give him something to eat.

It was a very large lodge that Morning Star led Scar-Face into, and furnished with belongings of the occupants. Night-Light, sitting upon her couch of fine furs, greeted him kindly, gave him food, asked him whence he had come, and for what reason he had journeyed so far from his people. He told her of his great trouble; his desire to be rid of his scar so that he could marry the beautiful girl of his tribe; and she told him to be patient, that it might be done. But when Sun was about to return from his daily travel, she feared that he might be angry when he saw Scar-Face in his lodge, and so hid the youth under one of her white buffalo robes.

Sun returned, but, instead of entering the lodge, he stopped at the doorway, and said: 'Ha! I smell a human being.'

'Yes. A good young man. We are friends. Do not harm him,' said Morning Star.

Sun then entered the lodge, went to his couch and sat down, spoke to Scar-Face, who had come out from under the robe. 'I am glad that you are here with us. Remain with us. I am glad, for the sake of my son, that you are his friend. He often becomes lonely; your presence will be good for him.'

On the following day, after Sun had started out upon his trail across the blue, Night-Light said to Scar-Face: 'As you and my son go here and there upon this island, there is one thing I want you to do: never let him go near a gathering of big birds that have long and sharp bills, for they are very dangerous. They have killed my sons that I had before this one. I don't want them to kill him.'

Scar-Face promised to do that. Several days later, as the two were at an end of the island, they saw a gathering of the birds in the water, close in to shore, and Morning Star said to Scar-Face: 'There they are, the bad birds that killed the children my mother bore before me. Let us fight them.'

'You must not go near them. I promised your mother to keep you away from them,' Scar-Face answered.

But Morning Star would not listen. He ran toward the birds, and they hurried ashore and came angrily toward him. But they never got to him, for Scar-Face ran in front of him and with his spear killed all of the birds.

They took home with them the heads of the

birds, showed them to Night-Light, and Morning Star told her that Scar-Face had killed all of the bad ones. Then was her heart glad. She hugged Scar-Face; said that he was a real son to her; and when Sun returned, she told him how he had saved their one remaining son from the long-billed stabbers. Then was Sun pleased, too. He said that Scar-Face had done a great favor to him and Night-Light; that he would never forget it; and offered to do anything that he could in return.

'Then relieve me of this scar; make my skin smooth, so that a beautiful girl of my tribe, that I want, will have me for her man,' Scar-Face replied.

'I will remove it,' said Sun. And he rubbed a black medicine upon the scarred cheek; rubbed it off, and there remained no least trace of the deep scar. He was pleased with this that he had done for the poor one. So were Night-Light and Morning Star.

But that was not all that Sun did for the young man. First saying that he was the chief, the ruler of the Above People, and of the earth and all life upon it, he instructed Scar-Face just how he and his kind should worship him, so that they might have long life, prosperous life, there upon the earth. The most important rule that he gave was that, each summer, a large lodge should be built in honor of him, and its center post hung with offerings of things that he most valued, and chief of them was the hide of the white buffalo, softly tanned. So many were these instructions for the welfare of the people that he was several nights in explaining them to Scar-Face. And at last, when he had finished, he led Scar-Face out a little way from the lodge, pointed out to him a long, white trail, told him to follow it, and he would soon again be with his people. Scar-Face started off upon it; the Wolves' Trail it was (the Milky Way), and it ended close to the camp of his people. He entered the camp, sought the beautiful girl, and she was glad to become his wife. He then gave to the people all the instructions that he had brought from Sun for their benefit, and they have been faithfully followed to this day.

II

THE TAIL-FEATHERS WOMAN MYTH

After Scar-Face, there was one other of our ancestors who was with the Above Ones in their island home, one named Tail-Feathers Woman, young, and very beautiful. Many of the young men of the tribe wanted to marry her, but, one after another, she refused them all.

Going very early one day for water for her parents' lodge, she saw Morning Star still brightly shining, and said: 'How beautiful you are. I would like to be your woman.'

One day later on, when she went out for wood for the lodge fire, a handsome young man suddenly came and stood before her, and said: 'Well, here I am. I have come for you.'

'Come for me? What do you mean? I don't know you.'

'I am Morning Star. You said that you would like to be my woman, so I have come to take you to my home.'

The girl looked at him more closely. He was the most handsome young man that she had ever seen. Tall he was, slender, and his clothing, of soft tanned leather, was embroidered with bright-colored quills in pleasing figures, and fringed with many white weasel-skins. She believed that he was telling her the truth, that he really was Morning Star. She had idly said that she would like to marry him, but now she was eager for it and said so, said it without shame, without fear. And at that, Morning Star took a long yellow plume from his hair and stuck it upright in her hair; gave her a branch of juniper from which trailed two spider webs. He had her hold the upper web and place her feet upon the lower one, and shut her eyes. A little later, he told her to open her eyes. She did so, and was surprised: she was standing with him before a beautiful lodge, and he told her that it was the lodge of Sun, his father, and Night-Light, his mother. They entered the lodge, and Night-Light, there resting from her night's travel, was pleased that she had married her son; she gave her at once some of her own beautiful clothing, and handed her a digging stick, saying that, in her spare time, she could dig wild turnips for the lodge; but she must be careful that she did not dig up a very large turnip that she might see, at no great distance from the lodge.

Sun came home from his daily journey across the blue, and was also glad that Morning Star had taken her for his woman. He was very kind to her, talked with her about her people, told her various things that they should do to honor him, to obtain his help in their various affairs.

When out digging turnips for the lodge — the family ate them frequently — Tail-Feathers Woman often stopped and looked at the one that Night-Light had mentioned. It was very large; larger than a person's body; of perfect shape;

it would of itself be enough for the family for several days; she was tempted to dig it up, but always resisted and went on.

There came a day when, pausing again to admire the big turnip, she wanted more than ever to dig it. She resisted the feeling, as always before, and went on; said to herself that she must dig it, went back, and stood before it; thrust her digging stick into the ground, but quickly drew it out, saying, 'I must not, must not do it,' and again went on. Again she returned to the turnip to dig it, and again resisted the temptation, more strong than ever within her. A third time she returned to it, and made a pretense of digging it; and then a fourth time. But this time, when she stuck her digging stick into the ground, she did not withdraw it; she could only push it in deeper, and then bear down upon it: up came the turnip and rolled off a little way. The woman looked into the hole in which it had grown; there was no bottom to it; she could see through it; could see, far below, the earth from which she had come; its plains and mountains and lakes and streams, yes, and the lodges of her people, in a big bottom of a river. She sat down at the edge of the hole, looked down through it a long time, looked at the camp of her people and became very sad: though she loved Morning

Star, she also loved her parents, and wanted to return to them, to visit them. She went back to the lodge, and Morning Star, looking up at her as she entered, said, 'You have dug up that which was forbidden; you have dug up the big turnip.'

Said Night-Light 'This is bad. I told you that you should not dig up the big turnip.'

The two did not speak to her again that day, and she did nothing but sit upon her couch and cry, longing to return to her people.

Sun came home, went to his couch and sat down, looked sharply at the young woman, and said: 'Something is wrong with you. What is your trouble?'

Said Night-Light: 'She has dug up the big, the forbidden turnip.'

'Is that so?' Sun cried. And then to the digger: 'Why did you do it?'

'I couldn't help it; something kept urging me to dig it. And then I looked down through the hole from which I rolled it, and I saw my country, the lodges of my people. I want to go to them, to my father and mother. I want to go to them, be with them again.'

'Go you shall,' Sun told her.

'No! No ! I love her. I do not want her to go,' said Morning Star.

'It is a great mistake she made, digging out that turnip, but that which is done is done. Now that she has looked down through the hole in which it grew, and has seen her country, her people in it, she will never again be happy here with us, and we cannot have that; looking at her unhappiness, we should be unhappy, too. She must go, my son, back to her people,' Sun replied.

There was nothing for Morning Star to do but let her go. Sun had a last talk with her; told her that she must not forget the things that she must have her people do to honor him and for their own long life and happiness. So was it that Night-Light gave her a headdress that she said could be worn only by women of pure life. Gave her, too, the sacred digging stick. Then Morning Star took her to the big turnip hole, tied a spider web to her under arms, and with it lowered her down to earth and close to the camp of her people. She went at once to the lodge of her parents, and they cried, they were so happy over her return; were very proud of her when they learned where she had been, and all that she had seen and done in the home of the Above Ones. And as Sun had told her to do, she gave them instructions in the various things that he wanted them to do for him and for their own welfare and happiness.

So was it that, from the knowledge of the Above Ones that Scar-Face and then Tail-Feathers Woman brought to the people, they first built a great lodge as an offering to them.

III

THE O-KAN´ (SUN DANCE)

Sun Dance is the anthropologists' term for the annual religious offering of the plains Indian tribes to their sky gods. The early fur-traders in the Northwest named it the Medicine Lodge, the adjective in this case having a spiritual meaning. As applied to the Blackfeet tribes' offering, it would seem to be the better term, for dancing is the least important part of its ceremonial rites. The Blackfeet name for it is *O-kan´*, and they say that the meaning of the word has been lost. Yet it seems to be sleep, or dream, for closely allied to it are, *ots-okan´* (his sleep); and *opûp´okan´* (his vision-sleep).

The Medicine Lodge, as we shall continue to call it, is the result of a vow made to Sun. With the Crows, Sioux, Cheyennes, and Arapahos, a man makes the vow, but with the Blackfeet it is a woman, for it was a woman, Tail-Feathers Woman, who, even more than Scar-Face, brought from Sun himself the request that the people should build it for him and his wife and son. So is it that, when a woman's husband, son, or other near relative is ill, or off to war and in great danger, she may, if pure and virtuous, publicly vow to Sun that, if he will make well the sick one, or help the absent one to survive all dangers, she will in the coming summer build a Medicine Lodge. If more than one woman makes the vow in the course of the year, it is the first one of them who is the real lodge-giver and the others are her assistants.

As of old, every summer, each tribe of the confederacy puts up a Medicine Lodge: the Blackfeet, east of Calgary, in the latter end of June; the Pikû´ni (Montana Blackfeet), July 1 to 10; the Bloods, July 10 to 20; and the North Pikû´ni right after the Blood ceremonies. Visitors in Glacier Park and in Watertown Lakes Park can attend the interesting ceremonies daily, as it is but an hour's drive to the Pikû´ni ceremonials, and less than two hours to those of the Bloods and North Pikû´ni, on their respective reservations.

The Medicine Lodge ceremonial rites of the four tribes differ somewhat, in a number of details. Anthropologists have recorded those of the Pikû´ni '(Montana Blackfeet), so we give herewith those of the Kai´na (Bloods), as we have witnessed them for several summers, camping right with the tribe the whole time.

In each of the four tribes there is a medicine roll, or bundle, named the Natoas (Sun-Turnip), which must be owned by the sacred woman who has vowed to build the Medicine Lodge. If she hasn't it, she must purchase it from its owner, the sacred woman of the previous summer, who then becomes her mother, and assists her in fulfilling her vow, teaching her such parts of the rites as she has to learn, particularly the sacred songs.

In the long ago, previous to the time set for the beginning of the Medicine Lodge ceremonies, the hunters brought to the sacred woman and her assistants one hundred buffalo tongues, which they cut into thin sheets and dried for sacrificial food; for Sun had said to Scar-Face that buffalo tongues were sacred food, his food, that the people must offer to him. During the cutting of the tongues, Sun priests, or medicine-pipe men, sat with the sacred women, and sang with them one hundred different, sacred songs. Nowadays, beef tongues are used in place of buffalo tongues, and, alas! in lesser number; but

[1] See Clark Wissler's *Social Life of the Blackfeet Indians*, Anthropological Papers of the American Museum of Natural History, for the most complete account.

otherwise the cutting rites are faithfully observed.

At the appointed time, the tribe gathers on the slope running down from the Belly Buttes to Belly River, and makes camp. A beautiful sight it is, the several hundred lodges, many of them painted with sacred designs, set up in a big circle upon the green slope. Within the circle are but three lodges: that of the Horns Society, a very large double lodge, with buffalo head paintings in black; near it, the very large, straight-wall lodge of the Matokiks (Gathered-Women), the women's society, in proof of which are their travois set up all around the lodge wall; and last, the lodge of the vow woman and her husband and the lesser vow women. This lodge is painted a deep red, Sun's sacred color, and just back of it is placed the skull of a buffalo bull. A small, freshly cut cottonwood leans against the rear side, and cottonwood branches surround the base, of the lodge.

As soon as the great camp is well settled down for the coming ceremonies, a sweat lodge is built in front of the red lodge, and within it, with proper prayers and songs, the vow woman and her husband, and her 'mother' and 'father,' purify the dried tongues for sacrifice to the Above Ones. Following this, the vow woman and her assistant vow woman begin a fast, in the red lodge, of four days, during which they are taught the Medicine Lodge rituals, the various and many songs and prayers, by her 'father' and 'mother,' who also open, with proper ceremony, the Natoas bundle which she had purchased from them. It contains skins of small animals, small sacks of paints, tongs of a forked willow, seven rattles, and, most important of all, a digging stick, and a headdress, copies of those that Tail-Feathers Woman had when she returned to the earth from her stay with the Above Ones. The digging stick is red-painted, and attached to its upper or holding end is a bunch of the outer shells of moose hoofs. The rawhide band of the headdress is of rawhide, but in the shape of a lizard, and fringed with white weasel-skins. From it rise tall plumes, eagle and raven tail feathers, and attached to the front of it is a small human image containing seeds of native tobacco. During the opening of the bundle and the transferring of it to the new owner, the hours' long, interesting rites, songs, and prayers of the ceremony are carefully observed, and afford a most interesting spectacle. Some of the songs are as effecting and stirring as the more profound music of Handel and Haydn. In all, there are seventy different songs of the cermony. In them, Sun is called Old Man, Moon is Old Woman, but their son bears his true name, Morning Star. The ceremony opens with the burning of incense, the participants purifying themselves in the smoke of the sweetgrass and singing:

I am searching for sweetgrass. Powerful it is.
I have found it, taken it. Powerful it is.

Songs 2, 3, and 4 then introduce the Above Ones, as follows :

Song 2:

Old Man is entering. Says he: 'Let us have a sweat lodge.'
Old Man says, 'I want a fisher. I want a white buffalo robe.'

Song 3:

Old Woman is entering. Says she: 'Let us have a sweat lodge.'
Old Woman, she says: 'I want a fisher. I want a white buffalo robe.'

Song 4:

Morning Star is entering. Says he: 'I want a sweat lodge.'
Morning Star, says he: 'I want a fisher. I want tail feathers.'

During the fasting and ceremonies in the red lodge, the great camp is alive with various activities. Ownership of medicine pipes is being transferred with impressive ceremonies, each different from the other, the purchase price of several of them running as high as forty head of horses, a number of new blankets, several guns, and a quantity of tobacco. And daily, in their large lodge, the Matokiks (Gathered-Women) Society have their secret ceremonies and their peculiar dances, the latter open to the public. Their drummers, who mark time for their songs and dances, are men. Every day, too, one or another of the bands of the Ikûnikatsiks (All Friends) Society has its own peculiar dance somewhere in the open; most spectacular of them the dancing of the Horns in their beautiful war clothes, of beaded weasel-skin, and scalp-fringed deer-leather shirt and leggings, and war bonnets of horns and eagle tail feathers; in their hands their eight-feet-long crooked staffs, banded with strips of otter fur and hung with eagle plumes.

The lodge of the Horns is the only one of the camp from which non-members are excluded. Many of their rites are extremely esoteric. To them is delegated by the sacred vow woman the actual building of the Medicine Lodge. During the days of her fasting, they bring from the cottonwood groves in the river valley all the wall posts, wall rails, and roof poles; they set up the posts and lay upon them the wall rails. The diameter of the structure is about sixty feet. The forked, sacred center post remains to be cut.

In the evenings, and until very late, there is

much praying and singing of sacred songs in the lodge of the Horns and in the red lodge of the sacred woman; and elsewhere much visiting and feasting, smoking and telling tales of the long ago. And until next morning, bands of Night Hawks, youthful members of the tribe, on horseback, weave in and out among the lodges, singing their various songs, some of them gay and high-keyed, others so slow and sad that they all but bring the tears to the eyes of the listeners.

On the fourth day of the encampment, the fasting and the ceremonies of the transfer of the Natoas bundle are completed, and preparations for erecting the sacred lodge continue. The members of the Horns Society build a shelter just west of the Medicine Lodge structure, and thither repair the sacred vow woman, her husband, and the former vow woman and husband. They go in single file, the sacred vow woman wearing her Natoas headdress, her elkskin dress, and on her back the sacred digging sticks. They all gather in the shelter and pray and sing, while they await the return of the members of the Horns Society, who, mounted on their horses, all in their war clothes, had left the camp in the morning for the river valley to get the center post for the lodge.

The Horns are accompanied on this occasion by two old men who have good war records.

The rite of procuring the sacred center post is one of the most sacred of the many ceremonies pertaining to the Medicine Lodge. None but the Horns themselves and the old men, formerly members of the Horns Society, may take part in it. Arriving at the edge of a grove of cottonwoods, a halt is made, and the Horns go into the grove to find a tree of proper size and forked at the right height for the post. Having found it, they send messengers to report to the old men, who approach and count *coups*, four each, striking the tree at the end of each one, and finally praying that, when cut, the tree will not lodge upon others, and that it will not break and split the fork when it strikes the ground. They assure Sun that, when the post from the tree is set up, they will hang presents upon it for him. Younger members of the society then cut down the tree, and all return to the Medicine Lodge structure, forming a long procession around the camp, singing as they approach the structure; and lay the center post with its butt end at the hole in the center of the structure, that has been dug for it, its forked end to the west.

All of the preparations have now been made for the raising of the post, and the people assemble. The women of the Matokiks, four of them dressed to represent buffalo, file out from their lodge and seat themselves northeast of the shelter of the sacred woman. The Horns Society members, all dressed in their best, come from their lodge, and sit to the east of the shelter, and face it; and in a great circle around, the whole tribe gathers.

In front of the shelter, a well-soaked beef hide is laid, and, with considerable ceremony, is cut into strands for binding the butts of the roof poles of the Medicine Lodge to its wall rails. This rite must be performed by a warrior who counts four *coups* before cutting the hide.

Owners of medicine pipes, after taking their elaborately decorated pipes into the shelter for prayers, pass them along the line of Horns and Matokiks, and give each one a few whiffs of the pipes, during which the smokers pray the Above Ones for long and full life.

Steps forward then the vow woman, the relative for whom she made the vow beside her, and both stand upon a robe while the sacred woman holds the dried tongue up to the sky, praying to the Above Ones, and breaks off portions of the offering and buries them in the ground with prayers to Earth-Persons. She then gives out a small piece to each applicant. Those who take the sacred tongue offer prayers as did the sacred woman; then eat the remainder of the portions.

Now the sacred woman faces the center post, and the Horns go inside the Medicine Lodge structure. One of their number, painted black, is stretched out full length on the post. Behind robes, medicine men perform a rite over him. He rises, and in his place they attach gifts which the people have brought as offerings to Sun. Then from north, south, east, and west advance large groups of the men of the tribe, converging upon the Lodge. They carry lodge poles tied in pairs, like long-handled tongs or pincers. They sing, as they advance, thrilling songs that belong to this part of the ceremonial rites, by turn advancing, stopping, advancing, until, at last, they reach the structure, and with their long prongs, amid the victorious shouts of the crowd, they raise the post and securely set it in the hole dug for it.

They set the tips of the roof poles in the fork of the center post, others pushing them up over the wall rails, and bind the butts to the rails with the strips of rawhide. The roof and walls are then laid with brush, and the people repair to their lodges. All of this must be accomplished before Sun sets.

On the following day, the Sun priest, whom the Horns have selected, enters a booth constructed of boughs opposite the entrance to the Lodge, and there offers prayers for good weather during the remaining days of the Medicine Lodge, paints the faces of those who come to him with gifts for Sun, and prays for the welfare of the tribe. The Horns distribute gifts to the poor, food in particular. On succeeding days, the societies continue their dances in the Lodge, and around the camp, until the tenth day, when all of the lodges of the great camp are taken down.

The last rite of the Matokiks attracts much interest in the camp. Before sunrise, they go from their lodge to a rise of ground east of the camp, and lie down. There they remain until some time after sunrise, when a man, a buffalo caller, approaches from the north, uttering the peculiar cries with which his fathers enticed herds of the animals to the *piskans* of the cliffs. The Matokiks suddenly sit up, stand up, listen to the cries, and when the caller is quite near them, they break for camp, bounding along like buffalo, and hooking at the people they pass, particularly the four women dressed like buffalo bulls.

All of the sacred ceremonies completed, the members of the tribe go their various ways, happy in the belief that their prayers and their sacrifices to the Above Ones have been answered.

Priests and preachers and contact with the civilization of the whites have made no least dent in that belief: they are as sure of it as are the Fundamentalists that the God of their faith made the world in six days, that Christ turned water into wine, and that Jonah survived three days intombed in the belly of a whale.

Long may they retain their belief in their sky gods, these Children of the Sun!

CHAPTER V

ORIGIN OF THE BEAVER MEDICINE

I

IN that far-back time when the various kinds of animals had the power instantly to change themselves into human beings and speak the language of humans, a Blackfeet man, with his two wives, left the great camp of his tribe, and set up his lodge on Sissukwoyi Ituktaki (Swift Flowing River; Bow River), where game was very plentiful; so plentiful that each day of his hunting was successful. One day, after he had gone out to hunt, his younger wife, a very beautiful young woman, went to the river for water, and was surprised to see a very handsome young man standing upon the shore. He was the son of Beaver Chief, whose underwater lodge was in a deep stretch of the stream, just below.

The young woman continued on her way with bowed head, and stooped to fill her earthen pot,' when she heard the man say, 'I have come for you.

'But I do not know you,' she answered, arising and looking affrightedly at him.

At that, the underwater man used his strange power upon her: unable to resist it, she consented to go with him. He led her down the shore a little way, pointed to a stone a little way out from it, told her to put her foot upon it, shut her eyes, and keep them shut until bidden to open them. She did as ordered, and, when told to open her eyes, was amazed to find herself in a large lodge of strange furnishings, particularly a large, decorated roll at the back of it. At the right of it, upon a couch of fine furs, sat the owner of the lodge, Beaver Chief, and on his right was his wife. The young man who had brought her there was their son. They told her that she was very welcome there.

When the young wife of the hunter did not soon return with the water, the elder wife became uneasy and went to learn what detained her. She found her tracks to the shore, the filled pot of water upon it, and then her tracks down the shore a little way and to the water's edge.

Returning to the lodge, the elder wife anxiously awaited the return of the hunter. Waited and waited; never had he been so long away. It was after dark when he came in with a backload of meat.

He at once noticed that she was alone, and asked: 'Where is your sister?'

'She went for water soon after you left, and did not return. I tried to find her, found only the pot that she had filled, and her tracks down the shore a little way, and to the water's edge,' elder wife replied; and did not dare look at him, fearing his anger. To her great surprise, he seemed not to be even worried.

'She must have a lover; likely he came for her, has taken her away,' he answered, and asked for broiled meat to satisfy his hunger.

When night came, the hunter's younger wife became restless, then terribly worried: What would her man think when he returned home and found her gone? What would he do in his anger? Would he beat her innocent sister?

Beaver Chief was watching the woman, and now he told her that her man had returned, had learned of her strange absence, and was not at all angry. This he knew, he said, because of his great power. And then he went on:

'You will remain here four nights; then leave my lodge and return to your lodge.'

'Yes. As you say,' she replied. She knew that four was the sacred number, and that her stay in Beaver Chief's lodge for four nights must have sacred meaning.

'On the fourth morning, just as Sun appears,' Beaver Chief continued, 'you will leave my lodge, but you must not enter your lodge. Standing outside it, you will know if your man is angry. He will be there at that appearing of Sun.'

'Yes, he will be there as Sun begins his travel, up in the blue,' said the woman.

'If he is not angry, you will call out to him, to his other wife, to burn incense for you; in two places: at the doorway, and at the back of the lodge, behind the fireplace. You will purify your body as you enter the lodge; you will purify it with the incense smoke before you enter the lodge. It must be done as I tell you.'

'As you order, so will I do,' the woman replied.

On that fourth morning, the young woman left Beaver Chief's lodge and went and stood before her lodge. But when she spoke, as she had been told to do, her sister replied that their man had already gone off to hunt. But she set incense at the doorway and at the back of the lodge, sweet-grass incense, and the returned one purified herself, first in the smoke at the doorway, and then, entering, at the back of the lodge. Then the two sat down.

'Is our man angry because of my strange absence?' the younger one asked.

'No. He does not know why you

disappeared; he is uneasy about it, but not at all angry.'

The younger wife was greatly relieved when she heard that. She told her sister of her wonderful experience in Beaver Chief's underwater lodge, and that she must at once return there, as Beaver Chief had promised to reward their man if he proved to be not angry at her four nights' absence. She then went down to the shore of the river and obeyed Beaver Chief's instructions to act just as she had when his son had taken her: she stepped on the stone a little way out from the shore, and almost at once was in that underwater lodge.

That evening, Beaver Chief said to her: 'Your man returned to his lodge. Your sister has told him of your visit with her, and of all that you told him. And she urged him not to be angry, because the people whom you are with are very powerful, very sacred.'

'And was he angry?'

'No. "I will not get angry," he told your sister. "How could I be angry when they are sacred people who have taken her?" And then he said that he had one great desire: that he might see you again.'

'What reply did my sister make to that?'

'She told him that, because he was not angry at you, you were coming back to him.'

'Is that, then, my return to him, the reward he is to have for all his worry about me?'

'That, and something else: something very sacred, something that will be very valuable to him and to all of his tribe of people,' Beaver Chief replied.

And a little later, he added: 'As always, at this time of early summer, the waters of the rivers are rising. Of all the lodges of us Water People here, mine alone is safe from the flood; so is it that those of the other lodges will come here for safety. You are to remain four nights longer, so that you may see them all, get to know them, learn their sacred powers, so that you may explain it all to your man when you return to him.'

Even as he spoke, the water was fast rising, and presently there came in, for refuge with the Beaver Chief, a Water Diver (Hell diver), then a beaver; and after it, one after another, all the water animals and birds.

When they were all gathered in the lodge and comfortably sitting, Beaver Chief said to them: 'I want you all to give this visiting woman here your songs, your sacred songs. Begin.'

The beaver that had come in was first to comply. The words of his song were: 'My old home [Beaver Chief's lodge] is sacred.'

The loon sang: 'My home is water; it is sacred.'

One after another, the various kinds of ducks sang the same song as the loon gave.

The otter: 'When I go into the water, which is sacred, my whistling is sacred.'

Now, while these birds and animals were singing, Beaver Chief was painting a large circular piece of clear [white] buffalo rawhide with representations of them. The woman wondered what it was for, but did not dare ask. She later learned that it was to be formed into the dish in which her people were to mix their sacred tobacco seeds, for planting in their gardens.

All those present in the lodge had given their songs, when the lizard entered, stood close to the doorway, and said to Beaver Chief: 'I want my body painted on that hide.'

'Ha! What is this thing doing in my lodge? He has no song,' Beaver Chief muttered.

'What? You say that I have no song?' Lizard shouted; and at once sang a beautiful song, in which were the words: 'My body asks for rain. Have pity on me.' He had no more than finished when rain began to fall right into the lodge.

That frightened those gathered there, and Beaver Chief, too, powerful though he was. He lit a pipe, presented it to Lizard, and asked him to stop the rain.

'As you say,' Lizard answered, and he

sang: 'My body asks for rain to cease. Have pity.' And at once rain ceased falling in there.

'You are powerful. I will paint your body on the hide,' Beaver Chief told him.

Then, last of all, Frog came in.

Beaver Chief looked angrily at him, and said: 'What is this nothing thing doing in here? He surely has no song.'

That time, Beaver Chief was right. Frog made no reply, jumped back to the doorway, jumped again, was gone.

Singing over and over the songs that the animals and birds had given her, the four nights were as one to the woman of the earth. Came the fourth morning, and Beaver Chief said to her: 'Get ready. We are now going with you to your lodge.' And then to his wife, 'Take it up, the sacred roll.'

This was the big roll that the earth-woman had noticed at the back of the lodge, and by the great care that was taken of it, she knew that it was very powerful, very sacred. She could not believe that it was to be given to her man.

Now, when the woman made her short visit to her lodge, she had told her sister, as Beaver Chief had instructed, that when she came again, after four more nights, the lodge must be ready for her, incense burning as on her first visit. Her sister had repeated this to their man, so now he was at home, anxiously awaiting whatever might happen. He had there with him in the lodge skins of every kind of animals and birds: one of each kind.

Now, as Sun appeared, the man set incense burning at the doorway and at the back of his lodge, and then, looking out, saw Beaver Chief approaching, then his wife, with a big roll upon her back, next their son, and last, his own young wife; and glad, glad was his heart.

When so near the lodge that those within could surely hear him, Beaver Chief brought his little following to a halt, and sang, 'My walking, it is sacred.' Then, moving on, and making a second halt, he sang, 'My halting, it is sacred.' A third halt he made, and sang, 'My walking, it is sacred.'

The fourth, the sacred halt, was made at the doorway of the lodge, and there Beaver Chief purified himself in the smoke of the burning incense, and, extending one hand above the other, sang: 'My lodge, when I enter it, is sacred.' He then made a feint of entering it, exclaiming, 'Ah´ha-ha-hai!' as one does when entering the lodge of a friend.

A second song he sang there: 'My lodge,

when I enter it, will be happy, and sacred.'
And again made a feint of entering.

Then a third song, with the same motions:
'My lodge, when I enter it, will have plenty,
will be sacred.'

And then the fourth and last song at the
doorway: 'When I enter my lodge, all is good,
it is sacred.'

He then led into it, went to the hunter,
sitting upon his couch back of the fireplace,
and handed him the willow tongs, red-painted,
and a small sack of incense, dried mass
(*Leptotenia multifida*), which he had been
carrying. Beaver Chief's wife then lowered the
sacred roll from her back, and laid it at the
hunter's left, just beyond the head of his
couch. When that was done, and the woman
had moved back, Beaver Chief made three
pretenses of lifting the roll; a fourth time he
bent to it, raised it, held it over the smoke of
the incense that the hunter had burning, and
sang a final song: 'This is where I remain. This
is where I remain. This place is sacred.'

Beaver Chief had now given the hunter his
most valuable, most sacred possessions.
(The hunter's younger wife taught him, later,
the songs that belonged to them.) In that roll
were the skins of the animals and birds that
had given her the songs, and also there was

the painted, circular piece of rawhide.

Now, as they all sat there in the lodge, Beaver Chief said to the hunter, 'You are to have more visitors, people the most powerful, the most sacred of all of us.'

Right then they were heard approaching the lodge; making the same stops, singing the same songs as those of Beaver Chief, when he had come to it with his family and the hunter's woman. And now the newcomers entered, and lo! they were Sun himself, Night-Light, his wife, and Morning Star, their son. Sun led the two around the lodge, stopping four times, and singing the songs that he had sung when approaching it.

Then, when the three were seated, he sang: 'I want various things. I want you to give them to me.' The hunter handed him some fine clothing.

Sun again: 'I want eagle tail feathers.' The hunter gave them to him; some very fine ones. Four other songs Sun sang. They were: 'I want other feathers; wings of birds.'

'I want a black wolfskin.'

'I want an ordinary wolfskin.'

'I want a white buffalo-calf robe.'

All of these things were given him by the hunter. It was then Night-Light's turn to request something, but she did not sing. Sun sang for her: 'My Old Woman wants an elk robe.' The hunter gave it to her.

It was now Morning Star's turn to make requests, but his father sang them for him, as he had for Night-Light. They were, first, 'I want a sweat lodge. It is sacred.' Second song: 'I want the skin of a fisher. It is sacred.'

Said Sun to the hunter: 'My first two request songs are not sacred, but the other four are. So are my Old Woman's one request song, and Morning Star's two. Seven sacred songs in all. You are always to sing them whenever you open this sacred bundle that Beaver Chief has given you: First, my songs, then my Old Woman's, and last, Morning Star's songs.'

Night-Light then said to the hunter: 'You are to include an effigy of me in the Beaver Roll. When you paint me, use black, for that color represents the night. You are to paint me, and sing all the songs of this Beaver ceremony, every time I newly appear. You are to use seven sticks to keep count of my winter new appearances. Not eight sticks, for my eighth new appearance makes the beginning of summer.'

Said Sun to the hunter: 'You will paint the seven sticks with black paint, and while doing it, you will sing my songs first, then her song, and last, our son's two songs.'

And with that, those three Above Ones went back whence they had come. That was the only time that they ever came down to earth and visited and instructed us people of the earth.

Such was the origin of the Beaver Roll, first and most powerful of all our sacred rolls. Later, as instructed by visions that he had, the hunter added several things to it: a raven-skin, lynx-skin, and buffalo bull scrotum. In those visions, appeared to him, in the form of human beings, first, Raven, who sang, 'The wind is my sacred element.' And a second song, 'I am looking for food; for a place to stay that is sacred.'

Sang Lynx, 'My head-hair ornament is sacred.' He had his own tail tied to the back of his head.

The hunter's last vision was of Buffalo Bull, who, appearing, gave him his scrotum, with which to make a sacred rattle; and also his song, 'When I go to water, I run.'

Soon after the Above Ones left the hunter's lodge, Beaver Chief and his family returned to their underwater home. The hunter then had his women pack up their belongings, load them onto the travois which their dogs drew, and they returned to the camp of their people. As soon as they were rested, the hunter invited the principal men of the tribe to his lodge. He told them all that had happened to him and his women, and for their benefit, opened his sacred Beaver Roll, with all the ceremonies pertaining to it. The guests were more than pleased with it all; they were very thankful that there was now in the great camp a medicine so very powerful, so sure to be of great benefit to the tribe.

But still the sacred roll was not complete. True, the hunter soon added to it, in accordance with his visions, the skin of the lynx, plumage of the raven, scrotum of the buffalo bull, but there were to come medicines still more powerful, as you shall learn.

II

A frequent visitor in the lodge of the returned hunter was a young man named Night Gun: an orphan; poorest of all the poor ones of the tribe. His one wrap was an old worn, round-cut, mangy buffalo robe, and because of it he was often spoken of as Scabby Round Robe. He was so deeply interested in the experiences of the hunter and his family that he never tired of hearing them related; and when in the lodge, he could not keep his eyes off the sacred Beaver Roll. The hunter's younger wife had great pity for him; more than liked him, and he had great liking for her. They were, as far as they could be, each the other's sweetheart.

In the river, not far below the great camp of the tribe, there was a large, abandoned beaver house to which Night Gun was strangely attracted; so much so, that at last he decided to pass his nights in it. Better that, he thought, than sleeping in the lodges of the camp, in some of which he felt that he was not wanted. One night, after he had occupied the lodge for some time, he had a vision. A Beaver Man who had owned this lodge, and was now living in a new one, near by, approached him and said, 'I have come for you.'

'Yes,' Night Gun replied, and followed him into his new lodge, in which were Beaver Man's wife and children. He remained with the family for some time.

One night, Beaver Man said to him: 'Why did you occupy my old, abandoned lodge?'

'I slept there, and in other places, many nights, trying to obtain a helpful vision,' he replied.

Said Beaver Man: 'You have now been with me a long time. I am going to give you power to strengthen your body. You are going to return to your people to-morrow. Look at my children and choose one of them to take with you.'

At that, Night Gun suddenly realized that this was no vision that he was experiencing; this was real. He was himself awake, and in the lodge of one who was undoubtedly Beaver Man, and the others there were his wife and children.

Beaver Man's wife had somehow taken a great liking to Night Gun, and she now said to him: 'When you choose one of my children, take the youngest one.'

'No. Don't take the youngest; he is of no account; take an older one, for they have more power,' Beaver Man said.

'No. Insist on the youngest one; he has the most power of them all,' said the wife.

Three times Night Gun asked for the youngest beaver, and was each time refused. But when he said a fourth time, 'Give me the youngest one,' Beaver Man replied: 'Take it. You are wise. The youngest one really is the most powerful of all my children.'

Said Beaver Man, further: 'You will start for the camp of your people early in the morning, as soon as Sun appears. Do not worry about the rivers along your trail, for youngest one will take you safely across the greatest of them. The days will be hot, so don't travel any distance without putting youngest one in water, where he can cool off, and get a little food.'

And now was Night Gun puzzled. He had rivers to cross; the days would be hot. He must be a long way from his people. How had he got to this place, this lodge, and when? Well, he couldn't understand it, but here he was, and he was going home.

Sun appeared, and Night Gun set out, carrying the little beaver. He came to various lakes and little creeks, where, following instructions, he allowed the little one to rest and eat. And then he came to Big River, just below where Bow River and Elk River come together. He thought: 'I am a very poor swimmer. I wonder what I shall do ?' He held the little beaver up, so that he could look out upon the wide, swift water, and hoped that he would help him.

Said the beaver, 'Get a log.' Night Gun rolled a big, dry drift log down the shore and into the water. Three times he attempted to put the beaver in also, but could not do it. But the fourth attempt was successful. The beaver went in willingly, took the log upon his back. Night Gun got onto the log, and the beaver towed it to the opposite shore.

So was it that Night Gun returned to the

Blackfeet camp, and soon afterward the little beaver died. Beaver Man had warned him to take great care of the little one, and he had done so, yet now the little beaver was dead. He had great pity for the little one. He thought that his parents would want him, so he took him back to them. Upon the way, at Big River, he tried his power, his sacred power: he three times lowered the dead little one almost to the surface of the water; at the fourth lowering, right into it, the little beaver came to life, and, as before and in the same manner, took him safely across to the other shore. And there, the little one died again. He went on quickly with him and arrived at Beaver Man's lodge. That powerful one had known that the little one was dead. He had told his wife that he was dead, and that the one who had taken him away was bringing him back. He was glad of that, for the little one would soon be again one of their circle.

'Ah! I told you to take great care of the little one,' Beaver Man said to Night Gun, when he delivered the dead one. 'However, I shall bring life back to his body. I am glad that you were but three nights upon your way here with him. Had your trail been four nights long, I could have done nothing; my child would have remained forever dead.'

In the lodge was a hole in the earth, filled with water, in which the family bathed. Beaver Man put the dead young one into it, and he came to life, and took his place with the other children. Then Beaver Man said to Night Gun: 'You cannot have the little one again. There are plenty of beavers. Get the hide of one, stuff it, and, whenever you so wish, it will come to life again. With it, its great power, be not afraid of anything, no matter how terrible it may be, for you will always overcome it. Now, you are going to return to your people.'

So was it that powerful Beaver Man favored Night Gun, had great pity, great love for him. His parting gift to him was a beaver-gnawed stick, which, he said, was to be his powerful shield.

Soon after starting upon his back trail, Night Gun killed a beaver, a small one, no more than two moons of age, and stuffed the hide with moss to make it look as lifelike as possible. He carried it at his side, suspended from his shoulder by a thong, and under his shirt, where none might see it. But, upon arriving in camp, he soon found an opportunity to meet his sweetheart, the hunter's younger wife, and tell her all about his trip back to Beaver Man, and show her the powerful medicines that he now had. He handed her the beaver-gnawed stick, told her to keep it carefully until such time as he would find use for it.

Not long after Night Gun returned, the camp crier announced one morning that there would be a costume dance that day. This was not a sacred dance. It was a dance of that far-back time, and was at last forbidden, because it created a lot of trouble among the people. In this dance, every sweetheart of every man, dressed exactly as the man did, and took part in it. You can see how that would cause trouble; much jealousy, especially among the married ones.

Now, Night Gun was poor; his clothing was so old and shiny and torn that he was ashamed to take part in the dance; yet he painted himself, cleaned as best he could his leggings and moccasins, and joined in.

When the camp crier announced the dance, the hunter said to his younger wife: 'I think that you have a sweetheart. I pity you; I pity him. Therefore, clothe yourself as he is clothed, and go and dance.'

Gladly, yet fearfully, the woman cut an old worn buffalo robe to a round shape, for her wrap. She stuck up a raven feather at the back of her head. She rubbed her hands with white paint and pressed them tightly to her cheeks, leaving the white shape of them there. So was she dressed and painted the same as Night Gun. She went to the center of the camp and danced opposite him. He heard people making unkind remarks about him; heard one say: 'That Night Gun is not much of a man. He has only a married woman for a sweetheart.' At that, he said to his sweetheart: 'I will prove to these people how much of a man I am. Hold up now the sacred, gnawed stick I gave you; dance with it, and sing the song that I taught you.'

The woman danced, holding the stick out and up from her body with her right hand, and she sang, 'When the waters are warm again, I am going to strike with this stick.'

The people knew what that meant: Night Gun was going to war. When the dance ended, he announced that he was going against the enemy.

The whole camp knew that he had been twice away, visiting the underwater people, and, too, his sweetheart was no other than she who had been the means of her man obtaining the powerful Beaver Roll. So was it that they believed Night Gun would be a powerful and successful war leader. A number of men, some of them much older then he, at once said that they would follow him.

That evening, Night Gun met his sweetheart as she was going to the river for water, and she returned to him the beaver-gnawed stick that he had given her to keep for him. On the following morning, he called his party together, and they started out, he in the lead, carrying the sacred stick in his right hand; and concealed under his shirt was the stuffed beaver-skin. At his side, wherever the way was clear, walked his one close friend, a young man named Fox Eyes.

The party traveled south for several days, and came to a wide and swift river, on the far side of which they discovered a large party of men, a long line of them standing along the shore, and one, their chief, well in front of the center of the line. At that, Night Gun's party scattered out along the shore, he, with his friend, remaining a little to the west of the nearer of them.

Now, as they all watched the enemy across, trying to make out who they were, their chief signed: 'Come into the water! Come over and fight us.'

'No. You come across and fight us,' Night Gun signed.

'No. You cross. Come quickly and fight

us,' the other replied.

Night Gun whispered to his close friend: 'Of all our party, I care only for you. I shall go across, kill that chief, and bring him right here for you and me to count *coup* upon him. But I will tell the others to go farther down the shore, as I may bring him out there.'

Having told the members of his party to move farther down the shore, as he was going to kill the enemy chief, and would probably bring his body out there, he signed to the chief: 'I, alone, will fight you. Meet me in the water as I near your shore.'

'Yes. I will meet you, kill you. Come!' the other signed.

Night Gun stripped off his clothing, and for the first time the members of his party saw the stuffed beaver-skin that he had carried concealed under his shirt. He quickly smoothed it over with real paint, red paint, slung the stick at his side, and, holding out the beaver, sang: 'The water is my sacred element. It is sacred.'

He sang a second song: 'My chief, Beaver Man, says: Water is my power!'

Then loudly, with courageous voice, the third song: 'I will try to go over there, and survive.'

At last, his fourth song — four, the sacred

number: 'I have survived. Beaver is watching me, taking care of me. He is of Sun.' And with that, he dived into the river.

When out about halfway across, he came up in sight, and then something very wonderful was seen by his party: he appeared to be walking onward, as though his feet were upon the ground; yet was the water very deep out there. And presently he signed to the enemy chief: 'Come out to me in the water.'

'No. You come to me where I am,' the other signed. And so lied; went back on his promise to meet Night Gun in the water.

Night Gun reslung the stuffed beaver at his side, took the gnawed stick in his right hand, and again signed to the enemy chief: 'Come to me, out here in the water.'

The chief shook his long, flint-tipped lance, and signed back: 'No. You come to me.'

But Night Gun persuaded him to come out; he cast a spell upon him so that he had to come. But he became frightened, stopped, then came on, stopped again.

A third time Night Gun, holding out the stick, said to him: 'You come.' And then: 'Strike first.'

By this time, Night Gun was quite near the shore, in not deep water. The enemy chief saw that he had no weapon, and waded out toward him, and with both hands cast his lance. But Night Gun was holding up his sacred beaver-gnawed stick. It was his shield. The lance glanced off it, glanced down, and stuck in the bottom of the river. Night Gun seized it, threw it, killed the chief with his own weapon, seized him by the hair of his head, and started back with him, still apparently wading and walking upon the ground, and leaving the dead one's party, crying, mourning for him.

Upon reaching the middle of the river, Night Gun dived, and his party, all but his close friend, Fox Eyes, ran farther down the shore to a point where they thought he would come out with the body. But instead of that, he swam upstream after diving, and brought the body ashore where his friend was standing. This enemy proved to be a chief of the Snake People, as was shown by the way his hair was dressed: a big topknot, and two side braids. Night Gun scalped off the topknot, and told his friend to scalp one of the braids. The others of his party came running to him, and he gave them the other braid: that is, the first two of them who arrived, they dividing it between them, for the killing of an enemy chief makes permissible the counting of four *coups*.

Nothing happened to the party upon their

homeward trail. When they came in sight of the great camp, Night Gun, in the lead, called a halt, and raised a hand to attract the attention of the people, and, as they stared at him, he looked back over his shoulder, the sign that he had been victorious. At that, the hunter, he who had the sacred Beaver Roll, told his younger wife, to go and meet her sweetheart. She was gathering rosebuds at the time, and, dumping them upon the ground, went running, went quickly to Night Gun and kissed him; told him that her man invited him to his lodge. She went there with him, proudly carrying the scalp of the Snake chief, and his lance.

They entered the lodge, and Night Gun said to the hunter: 'I give you these things that I took from the chief whom I killed.'

So was it that scalps were included in the various sacred things of the Beaver Roll.

III

The owner of the sacred Beaver Roll had a close friend who was also a great hunter. When out one day after meat, this friend came upon a female elk and her two children, and prepared to kill them. But as he fitted an arrow to his bow, he was surprised to hear the elk singing; and still more surprised when he heard her sing to him, 'You, earth-man, have pity on me and my children, for I am sacred.'

The hunter lowered his bow, and decided that he would not shoot. Then he heard a male elk coming. It soon appeared, and it was in the form of a human being, yet did it have the hump and the antlers of an elk, and it was singing a song in which were the words, 'I am looking for my woman.' Then the singer saw her, went to her, and they sang several songs; their children also sang. The hunter listened to them carefully, so that he would not forget them. Upon arriving in camp, he went to his friend, the Beaver Roll man, told him of the wonders that he had seen and heard, repeated again and again the songs, until the Beaver Roll man could sing them perfectly. They became a part of the songs of the roll, along with an elk war bonnet and hump, which were made later on.

CHAPTER VI

THE SACRED TOBACCO RITES

All three tribes of the Blackfeet formerly planted gardens of 'native' tobacco annually; but the Blood tribe planted it last in 1871, and no one can remember the last planting of the Pikû′ni. The Blackfeet tribe proper, alone, has continued the complex ceremonies associated with the planting of the 'sacred tobacco'; and from the interest shown in these rites at the present time, the tribe will continue the 'planting' for some years to come.

It is more than likely that the Blackfeet tribes obtained their first seeds of the plant from the Crows and witnessed their ceremonial rites in connection with it. Then they, in turn, modified the rites in accordance with their own cultural ideas. The Blackfeet ritual is much more elaborate than the Crow; and the Crow organization is much more complicated than the Blackfeet, which, in fact, has been kept very simple.

Although the planting of tobacco was practiced almost universally by the American

Indians, only the Crows, the Blackfeet, and the Saksiks (Sarsi) accompanied the planting with ceremonials, and the Saksiks almost certainly took over their rites from their allies and protectors, the Blackfeet tribes.

When our camp at Water Lake broke up, and our Blood and North Pikû´ni friends returned to their reservations, we journeyed north to the Blackfeet Indian reservation, fifty miles east of Calgary, and met there old friends of the tribe whom we had not seen since they last hunted buffalo and traded with us at our post on the Missouri River, about thirty miles above the mouth of the Musselshell River, in 1880-81. We went first to the efficient and kindly agent of the tribe, Mr. George H. Gooderham, at Gleichen, Alberta, and he gave us permission to go here and there on the reservation as we chose, and did much to further the object of our visit. He referred us to Napi Stumik (Old Bull) as the one most capable of aiding us in our quest of information about the *mahwatosis* (hard-smoke), or 'native' tobacco, and the rites pertaining to it.

Although it was forty-eight years since we had last met, the old men gathered in Old Bull's lodges remembered us well, and at once fell to talking about the buffalo days and of a certain white spotted buffalo cow that his cousin had killed, in that last winter on the Missouri. The cousin had sold us the soft-tanned, spotted robe, and we had paid a lot of goods for it; among other things, ten hundred cartridges, five blankets, ten pieces of tobacco, and, best of all, three small kegs of whiskey. He remembered that whiskey. It did not burn one's mouth and throat; it went down as smooth as melted grease; but it was very powerful in one's insides.

He became very sober-faced when we told him that we wanted him to tell us all about the planting and harvesting of the *mahwatosis*. All that, he said, was very sacred, too sacred to be ordinarily talked about. We explained that we wanted to write it all, not only to add to the knowledge of the whites, but for his own people, those of generations to come, who would not plant the sacred *mahwatosis*, but who would be glad to know about it.

He considered that for some time, and at last said: 'True. When we old ones die, those who come after us, those who are too closely learning the white men's ways, will not follow our ways. It will be good for them then to read about the sacred plant, and all that their fathers sacredly did with it. Yes, my friends, I will help you in this to the utmost limit of my knowledge.'

Old Bull is a prominent member of the — as we may call them — 'tobacco planters.' They are not a society, but are, all of them, close adherents of the Beaver Medicine, the owner of which is the head man, the leader, in all the rites of the Mahwatosis, as well as of his own medicine; and in the Mahwatosis rites, he is the chief Beaver Man.

On the day after we met Old Bull, we began work with him, and so continued day after day, until we had the whole story of the sacred plant. And when it was ended, he did something for us that the Blackfeet had never before permitted: he took us down into the valley of Bow River to see the sacred gardens of the plant, we the first whites who ever had that privilege. But of that, more later.

So here Old Bull begins his story:

I

Every spring we move to the river. We call the place where we put up our lodges, 'Camp where we will make the Kos´stan' — the rawhide dish for mixing the tobacco seeds. After we are there several days, we make a sweat lodge, for Morning Star asked for a sweat lodge when he went into the hunter's lodge, and said that it should be built before any of the sacred Beaver ceremonies were to be performed. Our chief Beaver Man (owner of the Beaver Bundle) asks four young men to build the sweat lodge and to do all the other work for the ceremonies to come. Two of these helpers go into the timber for firewood and other materials. They get twelve green willows and a number of stones. Chief Beaver Man says to them, 'You build it over there.' They make the frame of the sweat lodge with the willows, the opening facing the east, pile the stones in front of the lodge, and build a fire upon them; they then dig a small pit in the center of the sweat lodge, cover the framework with old lodge skins, and when the stones are hot, go to the chief Beaver Man and say, 'All is ready.'

The chief Beaver Man, the leader in the ceremony, takes willow tongs and some sweetgrass and goes to the sweat lodge; he calls out to the members of the Beaver Medicine to come. They all arrive and sit down beside the lodge. The chief Beaver Man enters the lodge, then invites the others to enter. All take their places, the chief at the rear, opposite the doorway. He holds a buffalo tail. He passes his willow tongs out to one of the helpers, and tells him to bring a coal.

The young man brings it in, following the course of the Sun (to the left of the fire), and places it in front of the chief Beaver Man. The chief Beaver Man puts the sweetgrass on the coal. He asks for the pipe. The I-pi-sah brings it, following the same course as before. He holds it before the chief Beaver Man, saying, 'Here is your smoke. We want long life and plenty.'

The chief Beaver Man takes the pipe with both hands, holds the mouth end toward the incense, and prays to the Sun, to the Moon, and to the Stars. Then he asks for long life for all the people in the tribe and that they may have plenty during the coming year. The I-pi-sah does the same, holding the pipe in his hands and praying at the same time. With a coal from the fire under the stones (matches are not used), he lights the pipe and gives it to the man nearest the door at the south. All smoke. Then they pass the pipe to the I-pi-sah, who is instructed exactly where to place it.

The young man is next asked to bring in the stones. He must use no metal, but a big stick like a forked stick, tied in the middle so as to hold the stones. He is asked to sit on the north side of the sweat lodge facing the fire, and to place the stick beside him. The chief Beaver Man begins to sing. He asks the I-pi-sah not to pick up the stick until he is told to in the song. He sings: 'Take a part of the forest. It is sacred [meaning the stick].' The young man picks up the stick. The chief Beaver Man asks him to walk toward the fire (outside the lodge) and to stop four times before reaching it. The chief Beaver Man sings, 'My walking, it is sacred,' just as the real Beaver Man did in the long ago, and after him the Sun, the Moon, and Morning Star. After stopping four times, the I-pi-sah is at the fire.

The chief Beaver Man sings, 'Just touch the hot stone with the stick.' The young man holds the stick in front of him, one hand above the other on the handle, thumbs up. He touches the hot stone with the point of his stick three times, the fourth time picking it up and starting toward the entrance. The chief Beaver Man sings, 'My walking, it is sacred,' the first two times, and, 'My stopping, it is sacred,' the last two times that he stops between the fire and the doorway.

As the I-pi-sah stands at the doorway, the chief Beaver Man sings, 'My lodge, when I enter it, is sacred.' And again, 'When I enter my lodge, it is happy. It is sacred.' The third time, 'When I enter my lodge, we have survived [as the Beaver Man sang to the underwater people].' Finally, when he sings, 'When I enter my lodge, all is well,' the I-pi-sah really enters the sweat lodge, places the stone at the south side of the hole in the center, brings in three other stones, placing them at the west, the north, and the east of the hole, without ceremony, and departs.

The chief Beaver Man breaks off a piece of sweetgrass, and gives of it to each member, asking them to put a little on one of the four stones, to take a little in the mouth and grind it up, and to put some on the head and body.

The I-pi-sah continues to bring in stones, the large ones first, then the smaller, placing them in the large cavity in the center. When the hole is filled, he adds the four stones to the pile, brings the vessel of water which the chief Beaver Man has requested, and places it on top of the incense. The chief Beaver Man asks that the door be covered. Then he takes a little water, throws four sprinkles on the stones, and asks the young man to lift the door a little (to let out the foul air from the stones). He sings:

> Old Man [the Sun] says, 'I am looking for a sweat lodge. I
> have found it.
> I will take the sweat lodge now.
> It is sacred.'

When he has finished his song, the chief Beaver Man asks the members which one of the animals in the sacred Beaver Roll shall be used in this sweat lodge. One chooses the buffalo, another the otter. So they sing the buffalo song, 'When I go for water, I run'; and then the otter song, 'The water is my power. It is sacred.'

The chief Beaver Man dips the buffalo tail into the water, sprinkles the stones, and makes a prayer: 'Here is your sweat lodge, Old Man, Sun.' He adds to his prayer a request for long life and abundance for his people. He selects a member, an old man, saying to him, 'you are to take this sweat lodge with Sun.' The member offers a prayer. So others, sometimes all of the members. If they want to pray, they do so.

We then go through the regular sweat lodge observances, without special ceremony. We make the stones as hot as we like, stirring the air meanwhile to circulate the steam. Four times we open the door, sometimes on both sides of the lodge. Then we are through.

The women never have a sweat lodge, not the Blackfeet. The North Piegan women have; but we were told by Sun that the sweat lodge is a ceremony for men, given by Sun himself. That is why only the men enter the sweat lodge. When we have completed the ceremony and have remained in the steam-filled lodge for some time, we go to the river and plunge into the cold water before returning to our separate lodges. Thus we are prepared to conduct the other ceremonies in the Planting of the Sacred Tobacco, ceremonies so old, so sacred, that only the Beaver Men, long trained in the rites, each the possessor of at least a part of the Beaver Roll, can take part in them.

Of the three tribes of the Blackfeet Confederacy, only the Blackfeet proper have retained these ceremonies, the Bloods not having seen the rites performed since Spuhts´i-kai-yo (Above Bear), when an old man, came over here to learn the Planting ritual; but one man can do little to preserve a ceremony. Not within the memory of the Blackfeet have the North Piegans or the South Piegans had the ceremony of the Sacred Planting.

But the Blackfeet proper are holding on to their sacred ceremonies. We are farther away from the white men. It is the white man that is robbing the Indian of his old-time life: of his religion, and his observances which were so sacred, so beautiful. Still have we three Beaver Rolls, the one given by the Beaver Man himself, now owned by A´po-pina (White-Haired Chief), and two others. These rolls are not purchased as are other Blackfeet sacred objects, by any one making a vow to Sun that, if his request is granted, he will buy a certain valuable object or privilege, but are willed to the man who is best trained in the performance of the ritual. He pays for it, but receives it as a privilege due him for the close study he has made of the Beaver ceremonies. A Beaver Man sometimes wills the Beaver Roll to an enemy. Men make vows to take part in the Beaver Dance in connection with the regular Beaver ceremonies carried on throughout the year. They give a feast to the Beaver Men and receive prayers, in the performance of the ceremony, for health, or recovery from illness.

The most powerful of all the sacred objects of the Blackfeet people is the Beaver Roll: so powerful that no white man dare approach the plot where the tobacco seeds are planted, lest he die. That is what happened to one white man. But later I will tell you his sad story, and that of an Indian who questioned the beliefs of his people; who wanted proof that the little images cared for the Planting, danced over the plot, and kept the tobacco seeds from harm.

Now I will tell you more of the Kos´stan ceremonies, of the making of the Rawhide Vessel for the mixing of the seeds.

When the women have scraped the rawhide well, we put it into water to soak. In the evening we gather in the big lodge, made of two lodges constructed as one, and sing the Beaver songs. Our songs are for luck to the seed which we will sow. When the skin is soaked, the chief Beaver Man sets a time for continuing the ceremonies of the Kos´stan.

The women, or sometimes the I-pi-sah-iks, go for the rawhide on a travois on which is placed a mat of cat-tail plants. The chief Beaver Man calls to all to come and see; but only the members of the Beaver Order take part. We bend a stick into a circle for the rim of the vessel.

All enter the lodge. The chief Beaver Man calls out from his position at the rear of the lodge for some one to get the rawhide. A youth goes to the travois and calls to those inside, 'I am right by the travois now.'

The chief Beaver Man calls: 'Take the rawhide. Bring it in the opposite way [that is, from north to east].'

He brings it in and places it on a mat or blanket. A container with white clay already mixed is near. The Sacred Beaver Roll has already been opened and rests in its place at the rear of the lodge, behind the fire.

The chief Beaver Man takes from the roll a Rattle, of Buffalo Hoofs. He rubs white clay between his palms and paints the Buffalo Tail, which he used in the sweat lodge, and the Hoofs. The other Beaver Men do the same. The Hide represents the Buffalo, was his gift to the roll. Singing his Beaver songs, the clay in his palms, he presses the skin four times, using the Hoofs to sprinkle the rawhide, shaking them in time to his singing. Then the skin is placed in the south of the lodge.

The chief Beaver Man then takes a Stick with a pointed end from the roll and ties to it a Top-Knot, that of the Snake Indian taken by Night Gun. He asks an old man to count *coup*, to tell a war story, then three others, at the end of each pretending to drive the Peg into the ground. When the fourth old man has told his story, he pounds a real peg into the ground with a hatchet. The Peg with the Scalp Lock and the Stone Hammer (a stone attached to a stick with raw-hide) are used as symbols in the ceremony.

Next to the Peg the Rawhide is placed, and near it, a bagful of grass. From the skin we cut rawhide ropes, then stuff the Vessel (the skin tied round with the ropes) with grass, and hang it on the Peg two or three feet from the ground.

The Vessel is about two feet in diameter. Hanging thus near the fire, it takes about four days to dry. In the mean time we paint on it the Lizard, Otter, Buffalo Bull, and the Raven. The lines, yellow and blue, represent the Otter's tail, blue symbolizing water, the Otter's source of power. Before the hide is dry, it is rolled over the circular wooden rim and sewn fast; and when thoroughly dry, the edges are cut smooth. All of this the chief Beaver Man does with the help of the other Beaver Men, never any one else.

The Vessel is now ready. It is placed on a tanned hide, and filled with the 'Buffalo Plant' (not identified, but so called because it bloomed at the time the buffalo were fattest), the bloom of the service berry (symbolic of spring), and other flowers, for luck from the full-blown plants to the tobacco seeds.

A rawhide string belonging to the Beaver Roll, wrapped in porcupine quills of different colors, is tied around the Vessel. From this are suspended a raven head, and other creatures from the roll: the red-winged blackbird, perhaps, or any that may be selected; and the Vessel, now completed, is put to one side.

On the day appointed by the chief Beaver Man for the continuance of the ceremonies, he, with all the other Beaver Men, starts singing in the morning. A feast is served, after which the singing continues; and the many songs of the birds and animals in the Beaver Roll are accompanied by actions, each Beaver Man having a particular part to take, until the man acting the part of the Buffalo dances, imitating at the same time the actions of the Buffalo.

Between the songs and dances of the different members, the Rawhide Vessel is passed to the man nearest the lodge opening, at the south. The chief Beaver Man sings his song. Each member takes an oval stone, and from four different positions, hits the rim of the Vessel. The Rawhide Vessel is the Buffalo. By striking it four times we represent abundance in food, buffalo meat, and good luck for the tobacco crop which is represented in the blooms. I myself held the Sacred Vessel at the last Planting.

This ceremony is followed by the dance of the man representing the Buffalo. The Buffalo Hoofs are thrown at him. He dances and carries the Vessel (the blossoms are removed) and the Buffalo Hoofs. All who want to dance behind him. At times he kicks at the people standing or sitting, pretends to be vicious, and causes much laughter. Each member possesses in his individual bundle three tiny containers, made of bladder-skin: one filled with the leaves of the tobacco plant, the second with the seeds themselves, and the third with seed pods. These they put inside the Vessel. The Buffalo Man finishes his dance. The ceremony is ended.

We pull down our lodges —the women do this — pack up our belongings, and prepare to move to the place where the seeds will be planted, the Tobacco Plot. With us we take a number of animals — buffalo in the old days, beeves now — in readiness for the feast and giving ceremony of the next camp. In this, our Rawhide Vessel Camp, our lodges are placed in long lines; in the next camp it will be different. I will tell you about it.

II

At the Planting Ground, we place our lodges, not, as in the Rawhide Vessel ceremony, in rows, but in a big circle, each lodge having its proper place. In the center, after the camp is established, we build the main lodge for the ceremonials, of two lodges together, but not until we have made a sweat lodge and held the ceremony there exactly as in the Kos´stan ceremony. The chief Beaver Man asks the I-pi-sah-iks (always men who have been sick and vowed to Sun to do this if they got well) to go to the timber and cut three long, green poles; and to get enough firewood for the night. Also to cut two logs, forked at the top.

The first night we paint an Otter yellow, and tie it on a lodge pole, singing, as we paint it, the Otter songs, four times each:

> The water is my sacred element. It is powerful.
> The wind is my sacred element. It is powerful.

When we have sung the many songs of the Otter, we carry the pole, with the painted Otter at the very top, outside the lodge and lean it against the tops of the poles of the chief Beaver Man's lodge. This we do the first night in the Planting Camp. Since the Otter is a water animal, he will bring luck to the planting of the Sacred Tobacco.

The next morning we erect the three green poles, tied together near the top with rawhide thongs, as a framework for the ceremonial lodge, placing the other lodge poles against these. The structure of the second lodge is adjoined to this, the two forming a huge lodge, oval in shape.

At the rear of the lodge sits the chief Beaver

Man, and to his right and left the other members of the Beaver Order. A hole, oblong in shape, is dug in the center; the forked pieces of pole, driven into the ground at either end, support a piece of pole above the hole, from which four pails are suspended.

The Otter is taken down from the pole on the morning of the second day, and is tied to a short pole and stuck in the ground at the plot where the tobacco will be planted. This is for luck.

A small poplar tree with many branches and leaves is stuck in the ground between the fire and the Beaver Men, and between the tree and the members pieces of service-berry wood are placed in a semicircle. The service berry is used because it is a spring plant, not like the evergreen trees, alike green the whole year around.

When these ceremonies have been performed, the lodge is ready, and we all leave for the Planting Ground. We sit near the Plot in a row, the men in front, the women behind. The Buffalo Hide from the Bundle is spread in front of us so that we can beat our rattles against it. The Rawhide Vessel is also placed in front of us, on the ground, next to the Otter; and beside it on the ground is the Sacred bundle, the Beaver Roll.

Opposite, facing us, sits the man who

carries the Loon on his back, and others who will perform a ceremony with him.

We sing three songs, led by the chief Beaver Man, who, at the fourth song, begins to dance with the Sacred Pipe from the Bundle. Next he picks up the Otter and dances with it.

Then the wife of the chief Beaver Man dances with the Forked Stick; and when she has finished that dance, she dances with the Peg from the Bundle used to hold the Rawhide Vessel. Four times she dances.

Next we sing the song for the Loon, and the man with the Loon tied to his back dances, now toward the members, now toward the Tobacco Plot, each way four times. He blows his whistle continuously as he dances.

The women follow with their dance, each holding with her left hand her own tiny tobacco bundle which she takes from the Rawhide Vessel, her right hand crossed over her left, as if she were holding a baby. In a line they dance around four times, when each woman approaches her husband and, with a prayer, offers him the tiny Tobacco Bundle. They pray for the health of all, and for the safe growing of the little seeds. Then they put the little sacks back in the Vessel.

Last of all the Buffalo Bull Man dances, with

the Buffalo Hoof Rattles. The wife of the chief
Beaver Man dances behind him, carrying the
Rawhide Vessel. The Buffalo Bull Man dances
where the women are seated, rattling his hoofs,
imitating the buffalo bull, trying to scare them,
and making everybody laugh.

The dance ended, all but the Beaver Men
return to the main lodge. A young man carries
the Sacred Vessel to its place, and another I-
pi-sah, after removing the Pipe, the Otter,
and the Beaver, carries the Beaver Bundle,
held open, to its permanent place in the
lodge.

III

Now comes the time for preparing the plot for
planting the seeds. Each of us forms a square on
the ground by placing four sticks as a border for
our individual planting. Inside this square, we lay
sticks side by side. On top of the sticks on one
plot the Sacred Pipe is placed; on another the
Otter, and on a third the Beaver. All of these bring
luck to the plots.

When we have prayed for health and plenty and
the abundance of the crop, we pick up the Pipe,
the Otter, and the Beaver, and set fire to the sticks
on top of our plots.

By this time the others have returned to

the plot and brought with them little switches of dry service-berry bushes. These they give to the Beaver Men, receiving in return prayers, and a gift of fat from the back of an animal, or tripe, which in this ceremony is sacred.

All, excepting a few of the Beaver Men, who stay to watch the fires, go to their lodges; and the I-pi-sah-iks return to the ceremonial lodge to prepare for the Food-Giving ceremony to follow.

IV

In his own lodge each Beaver member strips the bark off two little sticks, about a foot high and rounded at the top like a cane, which he has himself cut, and sticks them in the ground in front of his pipes, pointing toward the door. Each of us is supplied with a strand of sinew from the second stomach, also with service berries and cherries, the one with, and the other without, stones.

Carrying on our backs the food which we brought with us from the Kos′stan ceremony, or samples of things too large to be carried, we go to the main lodge and await the others. These stand at the doorway of their lodges, one after another calling out to certain Beaver

Men that they will make them gifts, that they will help them.

In return for such gifts, the Beaver Men make prayers as a reward.

Now the chief Beaver Man is ready to perform the ceremony. It is about sundown. He stands in the Sacred Lodge in front of the poplar tree, and sings, as the women carry in the food:

> She is sacred, the woman carrying food.
> The children have entered carrying food.
> They are sacred.

The people place the food in front of him, on the ground, and depart for their separate lodges.

Not until it is dark do they return to the Sacred Lodge. Then all of them come, so many that it is completely filled, for it is time to prepare the mixture: to cook the tripe, and pour the soup in the Rawhide Vessel.

V

Like all of the ceremonies connected with the Planting of the Sacred Tobacco, every detail of the mixing must be exactly right, just as it has always been done since that far-off time when our people were first taught how to do these things. Any slightest error in singing the songs, or in the order in which the various parts are performed would bring bad luck to the crop, perhaps to the whole tribe. That is why it takes so many years for a man to become a member of the Beaver Order.

When the people are all assembled, a fire is built the full length of the oblong hole, and the four Vessels suspended over it are filled with water; in the first vessel the Sacred Tripe is put to cook. An I-pi-sah stands on either side to watch, and when the Tripe is cooked, to carry it, with tongs for this particular purpose, to a mat of clean green wood on the ground.

The soup from the Tripe Vessel they pour into the Rawhide Vessel, and add berries, the chief Beaver Man singing songs as he pours:

> We are pouring them out.
> They are sacred.

He stirs the mixture with two Buffalo Ribs (not from the Bundle, but kept for this purpose). Flaying a Root (kah-ki-tan′) at one end to hold moisture, he dips it into the soup and gives each member, and his wife or wives, four tastes.

It is now late at night. The I-pi-sah-iks start cooking the meat brought from the Kos′stan camp, placing it in a pile when cooked. While they are preparing the feast, the Beaver Men sing one song and then another: to all of the birds and beasts in the Beaver Roll, sing until the food is served, at the same time hanging the Sacred Pipe, the Beaver, and the Otter on the poplar tree in front of them.

The I-pi-sah-iks feed first the Beaver Men and their wives, then the others in the lodge; and finally, if there are some who cannot find room inside the lodge, they fasten meat on sharpened poles that these hold in the doorway, and send it outside to them. It is almost morning when those outside the lodge have their feast. This is not a part of the ceremony, but has become the custom.

Each Beaver Man stands in front of him the two curved sticks which he prepared in his own lodge. The piece of second stomach he has soaking in a little vessel of water, and the sinew he has shredded, and looped at the end one strand which is as fine as thread. Pouring the water out of the vessel, he ties the piece of second stomach over the mouth, pressing it in the center to form a cavity. The tiny vessel he places in front of the two upright sticks.

All the members untie their individual sacks of tobacco seeds, those with which the women danced. The chief Beaver Man holds his seed sack with his left hand, and with his right thumb

and forefinger picks up a few seeds and gives
the same amount to each member, singing as
he does so

> We are pouring them in
> They are sacred.

Each member in turn does the same. The
wife of the chief Beaver Man dips her vessel
into the Rawhide Vessel, and pours some of
the soup into the vessels of the members,
giving each an equal amount of the soup and
berries.

Now the members tie their tiny
receptacles with the sinew and fasten them
to one of the sticks. On the other stick
there is nothing. After the members are
provided with soup and berries, the
remaining portion is divided among the
others present.

Mixing together pulverized buffalo and
antelope manure, the chief Beaver Man
gives each Beaver Man a small quantity, and
this, and the stick with its container
attached, we take to our lodges.

It is now dawn, and all go to their lodges.
There the Beaver Men mix the contents of their
tiny containers with the manure, in another
vessel, and retie the empty container onto the

stick. The second stick we stand upright in our own lodges. All is in readiness for the Planting.

VI

Taking with them to the Tobacco Ground the mixture, the stick with the empty container attached, and a sharpened lodge peg, the Beaver Men provide themselves with service-berry branches and with them sweep clean the burnt surface of their individual plots. They use the peg to bore holes in the ground, at least fifteen of them. Then into the holes they drop the mixture.

The women and children look on, around the edge of the Tobacco Ground.

When all of the members have finished planting their seeds, they form in a line, and the chief Beaver Man offers a prayer. He calls upon former prominent members of the Beaver Order, now dead, to come and protect the Planting. Four times he prays thus, each prayer to a different man.

The prayer ended, the women and children enter the Planting Ground and walk back and forth across the plots to cover up the seeds.

The little Curved Sticks, the members put into the ground near their plots, or on a tree in the Planting Ground, that they may protect the plots. Some of the Beaver Men leave Buffalo Stones on their plots as an added protection. This year, when the whole country around the Planting was hailed out, the plots with the Sticks and Buffalo Stones on them remained uninjured. Never in Blackfeet history has there been a time when the Sacred Plants did not produce seeds. Thus will it always be; as long as a few Beaver Men go through the ceremony without making any mistakes, the Blackfeet will have enough leaves for their ceremonial smokes, and seeds for the next year's crop.

Before leaving for their lodges, the members make a *piskan* (fence) around the Tobacco Ground to protect it from trampling by animals; in the old days deer, antelope, buffalo.

VII

Camp is again moved, this time to a spot away from the Planting. When the lodges are put up, in a circle as in the last camp, the I-pi-sah-iks erect a sweat lodge, around which the Beaver Men seat themselves and stand in front of them the second Curved Stick. A feast is served to the Beaver Men first, and then to the others seated outside the circle, after which the others leave.

The members go through the sweat lodge ceremony, the I-pi-sah-iks passing to them their Curved Sticks when they are seated inside the enclosure. They lay the Sticks side by side near the hole dug for the heated stones, and close the doorway.

When the chief Beaver Man has sprinkled the stones four times with the Buffalo Tail, the members pass their Sticks, sunwise, toward the entrance, where they are taken by the young men to the chief Beaver Man's lodge, the ceremonial lodge, and spread out on the ground behind the fire. The chief Beaver Man's stick is stood in the ground in front of his couch, and the others on either side in a semicircle.

After the sweat lodge ceremony, the members attire themselves in their ceremonial dress in their own lodges, and assemble in their accustomed places in the big lodge. Following the example of the chief Beaver Man, the members pick up their Sticks and, rubbing real paint, red, the Sun's color, in the palm of their hands, paint the little Stick, making it sacred. The chief Beaver Man sings meanwhile: 'Sacred Being. I am painting you with sacred paint.'

Four times he sings this song, holding in turn in his hand and rubbing with paint the Sticks of all the members.

Now the members prepare the Stick Images

for their journey back to the Planting. We tie onto them miniature moccasins which we have brought with us from our lodges; also a tiny bag of l'herbe (used for ordinary smoking), a little bag of punk, a tiny pipe, and a bag of pemmican. Some of the members put beads around the neck of their image. The curve in the Stick represents the head.

Now that our Images are prepared for their long journey, we sing songs, many of the Beaver songs, and finally songs especially to the Images. The women during this ceremony sit on the south side of the lodge. We give the Images to the women; some of the men prefer to hold them themselves. The chief Beaver Man sings to these little human beings:

> The Sacred Being [Sun] says, 'I have pity on children.
> They are sacred.'

During the songs, the women and men holding the Images swing them in a circle, round and round. Now the second song of the chief Beaver Man:

> Children, I have pity on them.
> They are sacred.

Each song he sings four times. By this time all of the men have given their Sticks to the women. The third song the chief Beaver Man sings faster, and the women dance with the Images around the fire four times, the chief Beaver Man's wife in the lead. Four times she passes the little Image to her husband, the others doing the same, and the fourth time he keeps it. When all of us have our Images in our hands, we offer prayers, and stand the little human beings on the ground again.

All of this time the Beaver Roll has been open, and now the three tiny bundles taken from the Roll are put back, to remain until the next year.

The chief Beaver Man dances with the Pipe, then with the Otter. His wife follows, dancing with the Forked Stick, all the other women behind her. Around the fire they dance twice, then the wife gives the Forked Stick to her husband, who puts it back in the Beaver Roll. The chief Beaver Man directs the women to remain standing. From the Roll he takes the Sacred Peg and gives it to his wife, singing while his wife dances around the fire twice with it, then the next woman and the next, until all have danced, and his wife hands it back to him to return to the Beaver Roll. Likewise does the chief Beaver Man's wife dance with the Beaver four times, then sits down with the other women.

Now the Loon Man, who sits near the door, is passed the Loon from the Beaver Roll, and dances with it as he did at the Planting Ground, the chief Beaver Man singing the Loon song the while. The other songs and dances follow in their order, always last the Buffalo song and dance performed by the same man who always takes that part. He is as comical as always, dancing with the Buffalo Tail and Hoofs, pretending to dig into the earth with his hoofs, and to charge into the women. A woman who dances with him pretends to fight back, and together they act out the antics of the buffalo cow and bull during the mating season. This is symbolic of fertility of animal and human life, and is a part of the prayers of the Planting for abundance of all life. When he is through dancing, the Buffalo Man throws the Hoofs at some one else, who dances with them, and passes them back to be put in the Beaver Roll.

The last dance over, the chief Beaver Man says, 'To-morrow we are going to send these little human beings home,' and all the people go to their lodges. A particular I-pi-sah is selected to take the images home.

VIII

The next morning the chief Beaver Man calls to the Beaver Men to hurry, to come to his lodge and bring with them branches of service berry with the blossoms on, each member to bring a fine flowering branch. We procure the branches in the brush near the river, and attach them to the poles inside the lodge.

Two horses stand at the doorway of the lodge, saddled, ready to take the I-pi-sah-iks over the hills to the spot near the Planting Ground where they will leave the little human beings, to find their way to the Planting themselves. Should they drop a single one, bad luck will come to the whole camp.

Inside the lodge we sing three songs; then all stand up, both men and women. We take the little human beings, and the service-berry branches, and sing, dancing slowly toward the fire twice, and toward the poles twice, making sweeping motions on the ground with the blooms, and exclaiming at the same time to instill in the image children the spirit of the earth. Four times we dance thus. Now we stand, the Image in one hand, the branch in the other, beating time as we sing (no rattles are used in this ceremony), and sing another song.

While we are singing, the two I-pi-sah-iks

jump into the lodge, one on either side, collect the Images and the boughs quickly, and run back to their horses, held outside by the other I-pi-sahiks, as if in a race, leap onto their horses and are gone.

The chief Beaver Man says: 'Let no one watch them go. Remain in the lodge until they are far away, and look not in the direction they have taken. To see them riding with the little human beings would mean misfortune for the whole tribe. Nor must any one seek out the hill where these little ones will be left, themselves to travel the rest of the way to the Sacred Tobacco Ground. To look upon them either on the hill, or at night in the garden when they dance over the plots and keep them from harm, would mean death, as it did to the young boy who did not believe what the old people told them.'

Everybody knows the story of this unfortunate boy, but the chief Beaver Man reminds them of it each year, so that others may not make the mistake that he made: how he doubted the story they told of the Images changing into human beings, and hid behind a hill near the Tobacco Ground, where he thought the I-pi-sah-iks might leave them. He watched them gallop up with the Images (the blossoming branches they had strewn along the way), stick them in the ground, the Image of the chief Beaver Man in front of the others, and gallop off again. No sooner were they out of sight than the Images turned into human beings. The head Image started to walk, and the others followed, their bags on their backs. Straight to the Planting they walked, boys and girls, and after dancing over the plots, took their places with their mates on the different Beaver Men's plantings. Not until he returned and told the people what he had seen did they know that the Images took the form of both boys and girls. But when he had told his story, he died.

While we wait for the riders to return, the chief Beaver Man tells the story of the white man who died as a result of having gone to the Planting. No white man is permitted to look on this sacred thing. This man was a stockman who was looking after his stock near the Tobacco Ground. He returned, and reported to the chief Beaver Priest that there were no plants growing in the garden. The Beaver Man knew better. Never has the Sacred Tobacco failed to grow and mature. When the members of the Beaver Order went to the Planting Ground to harvest their seeds and pods and leaves, they found the plants erect and plentiful. But of course they had hidden from the white man. That is why he thought the tiny seeds had not grown into plants. The Beaver Priest told the white man never to go there again. But he did. He wanted to make sure that no plants were growing. Not long afterward, only a few months, he was thrown from his horse, his neck was broken, and he died. Strange it was that this man, who was a remarkable rider, an old stockman, should have come to his end in this way.

His story ended, the two horsemen come galloping up to the lodge entrance, and the chief Beaver Man tells us all to go to our lodges, pack up our belongings, and prepare to return to our homes. The Planting-of-the-Sacred-Tobacco ceremonies are ended.

Thus Old Bull told us his story. Never once had he risen from his seat beside the fire during the course of his narrative. To do so would bring bad luck to the tobacco plants.

To our amazement, when we again visited his lodge the day after the last of the rites of the Tobacco Planting had been revealed to us, Old Bull told us that he and one other Beaver Man would be visiting the Tobacco Garden that very day, and invited us to go with him. No white man had ever been taken to the Planting, he told us; but because he believed that the work we were doing would be of value to coming generations of Blackfeet, he wanted us to go to the plot. The harvesting of the crop would not come until later.

Many miles we traveled over hills where only a trail was visible, finally coming to a halt on a hill sloping precipitately to the river below. Here we were told to remain until the Beaver Men returned.

After long waiting, we heard a call below, and saw Old Bull beckoning us to join them. There they were, little plots, each with its two bent figures side by side at one end; several with buffalo stones on the ground, or standing against the images. Bushes and trees grew around the plots, and all were enclosed by a fence. On every plot grew tobacco plants, very low this year, for the hail had struck the country when the plants were small; but it had not destroyed the crop, nor prevented the plants from bearing seeds. Strangely enough the plots with buffalo stones on them had the most abundant crops. Old Bull said it is always that way. On trees hung several rawhide vessels of past years, the paintings still distinct, the vessels distorted from exposure to the rains and snows of this north country.

Reverently the Beaver Men examined each plot, then turned and slowly trudged up the steep hill; two old-time Indians, the conditions of their external lives distorted like the leather in the rawhide vessels, the radiance of memory as vivid as the paintings of the otter and the raven. When we left them, on our return to the camp, Old Bull urged us to return in the spring, during the month of May, and join them in their Sacred Tobacco ceremonies. He even told us that we might take part in certain of the rites. It was with reluctance that we left the camp of the North Blackfeet. Here the spirit of the past seems to cling with a fierce tenacity. Not many years now until such men as Old Bull will be gone, and the younger generation will forget.

CHAPTER VII

WAR

ANTHONY HENDRY, in 1754, and Matthew Cocking, in 1772, were enthusiastic about the friendliness of the Blackfeet tribes. But in 1808, Henry stated in his 'Journal':

> The principal occupation of the Slaves [Blackfeet] is war.... Painted Feather's band are the most civilized, and well disposed toward us. The Cold band are notoriously a set of audacious villains. The Bloods are still worse, always inclined to mischief and murder. The Piegans are the most numerous and best disposed toward us of all the Indians of the plains. They also kill beaver. The other tribes stand in awe of them, and they have frequently offered us their services to quell disturbances made by other tribes.... At present our neighbors [Hudson's Bay Company] trade with about two-thirds of the Blackfeet, and I would willingly give up the whole of them. Last year, it is true, we got some beaver from them; but this was the spoils of war, they having fallen upon a party of Americans on the Missourie, stripped them of everything, and brought off a quantity of skins.

Before they began obtaining horses, the Blackfeet were doubtless at peace with the various tribes living upon the borders of their Saskatchewan country, and were not making war upon tribes more remote. But that condition ended with the very first horse that they obtained. They at once wanted more of the valuable animals; more and more of them; the elk-dogs that they could ride, load with their belongings, and go whither they would with ease; and to obtain them in any numbers, they had to make war, upon their owners. Long before Hendry met them, they were raiding horse-owning tribes far to the south; even the Spanish settlers in what is now New Mexico. With plenty of horses for transportation purposes, and with guns that they obtained from the British fur companies, they swept down and wrested from the Crows a vast and rich game country, the southern boundary of it the Yellowstone River. They drove the Shoshonies and other tribes into and across the Rockies, and held the Assiniboins and other Siouxan tribes at bay well to the east of them. They killed and plundered the American traders and trappers of the early part of the nineteenth century, incited thereto by the British fur companies, and at times were hostile to them also, killing some of their men, and destroying several of their forts. But they were ever friendly, except for good cause to be otherwise, to the white men who married into their tribes.

'War seems to be the Piegans' sole delight; their discourse always turns upon that subject; one war-party no sooner arrives than another sets off. Horses are the principal plunder to be obtained from the enemies.' Thus Alexander Henry, 1808. He might with equal truth have said it of the other tribes of the Confederacy, and their ally, the Gros Ventres tribe. And so it was with them all up to the extermination of the buffalo, in the early 1880s.

Soon after they obtained horses and met with more southern tribes, the Blackfeet observed their warrior societies, and, copying three or four of them, in time instituted a number of others of their own, until the Ikûnah´katsi (All Friends) Society in each of the three tribes, numbered twelve different bands: the Little Birds, Braves, Pigeons, Mosquitoes, All Crazy Dogs, Raven Carriers, Tails, Dogs, Seizers, Kit Foxes, Horns, and Bulls. In each of the tribes, some of the bands are still extant. Of the more powerful, more esoteric of them, the Blackfeet (Alberta) still have the Kit Foxes, and the Bloods, the Horns.

Each of these bands had its own songs, dance steps, and dance costumes, and its own ceremonial rites. The lodges of the leaders of the bands always stood within the great circle of the camp, and were headquarters and lounging-places for the members. The most spectacular of the bands was that of the Bulls, the members of which, all of them old men, in their dances and ceremonial rites, wore buffalo head war bonnets and buffalo robes, and imitated the ponderous movements of that huge animal.

The younger and unmarried members of these All Friends bands, when at home, were veritable sheiks. They worked not, neither did they spin. They didn't even hunt or trap, or herd their own and their parents' horses. They arose rather late in the morning, went to the river to bathe, and after the morning meal which their mothers set before them, they carefully combed and braided their long hair, put on their clean, spotless shirt, leggings, and wrap, beautifully embroidered moccasins, and with bow-and-arrows case slung to one shoulder, shield suspended from left elbow, and looking-glass in wooden frame dangling from their right wrists, they went outside and stood for hours like so many statues, their eyes apparently vacant, but actually alert for every young woman that passed their way. Their female relatives worshiped them, waited upon them with slave-like devotion. Their fathers amusedly tolerated them; they had themselves once been sheiks. So did they pass their mornings. Later in the day, they embarrassedly showed themselves in the lodges of pretty girls, or visited one another, and in the evenings repaired to the lodges of their leaders, there to smoke, gossip, sing the songs of their bands, and talk again of going to war. One or another of the great and successful warriors of the tribe was organizing a party to go against this or that enemy tribe, and they eagerly sought permission to accompany him. That granted, they were more than restless until the start was made.

Before becoming a member of the All Friends Society, every young man went to some place remote from the camp, a high hill, a cliff, an island, or lake shore, and there endured a long fast in order to obtain a sacred helper. Faint from hunger and thirst, in his sleep his shadow (soul or spirit) left his body and had strange adventures; met some animal or bird that promised to be his protector. He awakes. He gives thanks to Sun, Night-Light, and Morning Star: they have helped him; through his prayers to them they have brought about his wonderful vision. He staggers happily home to recuperate; he feels that he is now a man.

The leader of a war party was, quite often, himself a Sun priest, or medicine man, and generally had his sacred paraphernalia on his raids, carried by a youthful helper, a beginner in the ways of war. But medicine man or not, before starting out, he called upon some old Sun priest to officiate in a good-luck ceremony for him and the members of his party. They built a sweat lodge, and having all gathered in it, the old man had them assist him in performing all the peculiar ceremonies of his medicine, in which he prayed for their success against the enemy and their safe return. In conclusion, he passed his pipe, and each member of the party drew a few whiffs from it, to the Above Ones, to Earth Mother, and begged them to assist him in counting *coups* upon the enemy and obtaining many horses. Before entering the sweat lodge, each member of the party made a sacrifice to Sun, something of his belongings of value, which he tied to the branch of a tree or bush, with appropriate prayer. And at the end of the sweat, the party went to the river and bathed, dressed, and were then ready to start out upon their raid.

Experiences of war parties were many and varied. At each stop the leader slept apart from the others, and endeavored to obtain a vision (dream) that would reveal what the future had in store for them. The other members also prayed:

to the Above Ones, and to their sacred animal or bird helpers, for revealing visions. It sometimes happened that one or another of the party would have a vision that so plainly indicated misfortunes ahead that he and others, even the whole party, would about-face and return home. But if all continued favorable, the party kept on and on, with every possible precaution against discovery, and in due time found and raided the camp of the enemy that they sought.

In succeeding chapters are war-trail tales of several of our old friends that, we think, well illustrate the subject.

CHAPTER VIII

WEASEL TAIL

One of my closest Indian friends is Ä´puk-soyîs (Weasel Tail), a member of the Blood tribe of the Blackfeet Confederacy, and now seventy-two years of age. Away back in the buffalo days, in the Bear Paw Mountains, on the Judith River, and down on the Musselshell River, near its confluence with the Missouri, we had many a hunt together, and killed all we wanted of the game animals of the country, including several very large and angry grizzly bears.

A quiet, thoughtful man is Weasel Tail, owner of a sacred pipe, and wise in the religious and secular lore of his people. And as a member of the Horns Society, he always has a prominent part in the ceremonies of the Okan´ (Sun's Lodge), which his tribe annually builds in honor of that great and powerful 'traveler of the blue.'

Last summer, as usual, the tribe built the sacred lodge upon a gentle, green grass slope just under Belly Butte, and when the ten days of ceremonies ended, a number of us old ones packed up our belongings and repaired to Waterton Lakes National Park, there to camp together for a time, as is our custom, and, around our lodge fires, recall our adventures in the days before the whites swarmed out upon our plains and fenced in our hunting trails. And other talk we had; at night; after Sun had set: talk of the wondrous doings of the gods, tales not to be told in the clear light of day lest the teller be stricken blind.

Four large lodges and three small ones made up our camp there at the side of Istsipt Omuksikimi (Little Inside Lake), or, as the whites have named it, Waterton Lake, and in them we were: Weasel Tail, Big Wolf, Wounded-on-Both-Sides, Eagle Plume, Heavy Shield, Many Mules, Big Feet, Running Coyote, Spotted Wolf, Old-Man-Running-Around, and White Wolf; and Leaning-Over-Butchering, a North Pikû´ni, their women, and myself.

We had many visitors; tourists who were stopping at the Prince of Wales Hotel, upon the hill just above our camp. They came, many of them, from idle curiosity, just to see us and our camp; but they stopped to hear the tales that were being told, Percy Creighton, a mixed blood, interpreting, and they became interested; came again and again to listen; and so learned that

these native Americans were real, worth-
while people, instead of the lazy, immoral,
ignorant wretches of popular belief.

Day after day and evening after evening, I
recorded the tales that were told, and so in the
end had quite complete records of my friends'
adventures. Weasel Tail's account of some of
his war trails, which he told bit by bit, is as
follows:

'In the summer following my eighth winter,
my tribe traded their furs and buffalo robes
to the Hudson's Bay Company, at its post on
Bow River, and then moved down that stream
to camp, and kill buffalo for food and leather
for new lodges. There one of the men, Crow
Eagle, became dissatisfied with the hunting,
and said that he was going with his family
where game would be more plentiful. Our
head chief, Bull Necklace, strongly advised
him to remain where he was; to go off by
himself, he said, would be very dangerous, as
enemy war parties were everywhere abroad.
But Crow Eagle would not listen to the chief;
he said that he was well able to care for his
family, and, with his three wives and eight
children, he went south and camped on Rope-
Stretched-Across Creek [Lee's Creek], in the
midst of vast herds of buffalo.

'Came a day when Crow Eagle did not go out hunting until late in the afternoon, and then on his way home, he frightened a herd of buffalo in which he saw a sacred white one, a yearling. It was then nearly night, the horse he rode was slow, so he went on home with the meat that he had, and early the next morning, mounted his fast buffalo runner, and went in search of the white one. He rode about all day long, but did not find the animal, and night came before he neared his camp. From the rim of the valley he looked down upon it, and at once knew that something was wrong, for he could see no red glow of his lodge. He hurried down and found only the bare poles of it: the lodge skin was gone, and all that it had contained, and lying here and there near it were his three women and six of his children; dead, all of them, and stripped of their necklaces, bracelets, and rings. In his grief he wept loudly, naming them one by one, and from the near brush a seventh child, a little girl, came limping, and told him that she came from her elder sister, very badly wounded. He asked who had done the killing of his loved ones, and she replied that a war party of River People [Pend d'Oreilles] were the murderers. He hurried to the other surviving little girl, and found her very badly

wounded. As quickly as he could, he laid the
dead side by side, covered them with brush
and stones as best he could, attached a travois
to his horse, set the two girls upon it, and
started for our camp on Bow River.

'I saw Crow Eagle coming into our camp
with the surviving two of his family, and, with
many others, I hurried to meet them. We
surrounded them, and, even as he was crying
and telling us of his loss, one of the little
girls, gasping for breath, dropped from the
travois and died as she struck the ground.
And at that I cried: cried and cried. And there
and then, before that crowd of our people, I
called upon Sun to hear me: I vowed that I
would avenge the death of that poor little
girl; that I would make the River People cry
for what they had done to her. I was then but
eight winters of age.

'Winters and summers came and went,
and I did not forget my vow. In the summer
after my seventeenth winter, when we were
encamped right here at this lake, I went up
onto this mountain, this one which we have
since named in honor of our one-time
great warrior, Pinukwiim [Far-Off in
Sight], and there fasted and prayed for a
vision. On the fourth night of my fast, my
prayers were answered. Appeared to me, to my

shadow, as, it seemed, I was wandering along a river, a water animal, an otter, and told me that it would be my sacred and powerful helper, and advised me all that I must do always to retain its favor. So was it that, before winter came, I was enabled to join the Little Birds Band of the All Friends Society, and became, therefore, eligible to join a party going against our enemies.

'But I was to fulfill my vow before going upon a war trail. Early in the next, my eighteenth summer, we made camp on Old Man's River, near where Fort Macleod now stands, and from there, one day, my friend, Fox Head, and I went to hunt waving tails [whitetail deer] in the timbered bottoms of We-Fought-the-Kutenais River [Waterton River]. On this river, long before my time, my tribe had a battle with a large war party of the Kutenai tribe, and killed many of them; hence its name.

'My friend and I rode through two timbered points without success, and were crossing a grassy ridge to hunt in the next grove above, when, just as we neared the top of the ridge, a lone enemy suddenly appeared, riding down at us from the top, shouting his war cry, and saying in our own language: "Nistoa Nietuktai Tupikwan. Kitaks inita!" [I am a River People man. I shall kill you.] He fired at us, and killed my friend's horse, then turned and rode off the way he had come, I after him on my good horse. I followed him a long way, slowly gaining upon him. He fired back at me several times, but my sacred animal helper turned aside his bullets. He saw then that I had powerful medicine; that his bullets could not harm me. He began to shout back to me to pity him. I did not reply. When I thought that I was near enough to him to surely hit him, I fired; my bullet struck him in the back of his neck; he was dead when he struck the ground. I took his scalp, his blanket and gun, his horse, and two eagle-tail feathered bands that he had worn upon his head. So did I fulfill the vow that I had made in my eighth summer; so I avenge the death of that one for whom I had cried, that little daughter of Crow Eagle.

'Before the end of the moon in which I killed this enemy, I took a woman, and acquired a lodge of my own. I had long wanted this woman, and she had wanted me for her man. After I proved that I was a fighter, her parents were glad to give her to me.

'Came the next, my nineteenth summer, and six of us went to raid the enemy. We were Walking Star, Short Man, Camp Chief, Lone Rider, my woman, and myself. Leaving Belly River, we went south to the Sweetgrass Hills; from them to Bear Paw Mountains, then along the south side of Wolf Mountains [Little Rocky Mountains], and finally approached the junction of Little River [Milk River], and Big River [Missouri River], and I went on discovery; went on ahead of my party. I rode up a steep little hill not far above the junction of the rivers, and at the top of it came face to face with a Sioux rider. He thought that I was a member of his or some other Sioux tribe, and reached out to shake hands with me. But as our hands clasped together, the wind blew back the hood of my blanket capote, and he knew at once, by the way my hair was dressed, that I was a Blood man, and an enemy. He tried to draw away his hand, but I would not release it. He had a six-shooter strapped to his right hip and a rifle in a sling at the horn of his saddle. I had a six-shooter at my left hip and a rifle slung to the right side of my saddle. He tried to take my six-shooter with his left hand, and in the struggle we slipped from our horses to the ground. He jerked his right hand free from mine, and at the same time saw my party riding swiftly toward us. He knew that we were too many for him to fight; he did not even attempt to draw his six-shooter to kill me; he turned and ran down the hill toward the river, and the thick brush and timber bordering it. I quickly got out my six-shooter, took careful aim at him, fired, and killed him. Before my party arrived, I had his scalp, his six-shooter, horse, and rifle.

'We knew that the Sioux camp was not far away; probably in the big bottom where the two rivers came together. We dared not approach it in the daytime, so turned back a way, and then to the south, intending to go into a big grove of cottonwoods in a river bottom, and remain there until night. As we entered the bottom, we discovered eleven riders coming down it; nine men and two women. They thought, of course, that we were members of their tribe going out to hunt. We rode toward them, and, when we thought that we were near enough, we charged at them, shooting, and shouting our war cry. They turned and made for the timber, and we dropped one of them, a man, and Walking Star stopped to count *coup* upon him, take his horse and weapons. The others, six of them, rode into the timber and out of our sight, and four were so frightened that they sprang from their horses and ran into it. We took the four horses, and, knowing that the whole Sioux tribe would soon be after us, we struck out for the Wolf Mountains and home as fast as we could ride. We were not pursued. In due time we arrived home, and without further adventure.

'I have been on many, very many raids upon enemy tribes, and have, on ten of them, counted one or more *coups*. If, on the other raids, I neither killed an enemy nor captured enemy horses, I at least survived all the dangers that we encountered and returned in safety to my people. I attribute my success in war, my safety of person, first, to the animal of my vision, that water animal, the otter. A powerful protector, also, was a small bunch of sagehen tail feathers that my father had always worn when going to war. When he died, my grandmother put away the sacred bunch, kept it for me, and gave it to me when I first went against the enemy. I always wore it, as had my father, tied to my hair high up at the back of my head. Again, when I went on horseback to seek the enemy, I always painted and decorated the horse as old Eagle Child, a very powerful Sun priest, had taught me to do. Said he, when I went to him about it: "This you will do to prevent the bullets and the arrows of the enemy hitting you or your horse. You will paint the horse's right

shoulder and right hindquarter with red dots.
Why? Because, when you shoot a bullet
through the flame of a fire, the flame is not
injured, not even touched by the bullet; and
red paint represents the color of the fire
flame. You will paint the horse's left shoulder
and left hindquarter with white clay spots.
Why? When you shoot a bullet or arrow
through the smoke of a fire, the smoke is not
injured nor touched; therefore, the white dots
upon your horse represent smoke, and that
gives you the power of smoke, you and your
horse, even as the red dots give you the power
of fire flame, to be unhurt by the bullets and
arrows of the enemy.

'Also, there were certain things to be
closely observed when going against the
enemy. If any one of us dreamed that he saw
some one of our tribe killed, it meant that
we should go straight back home, for to go
on would mean death of some or all of us.
Another dream that gave the same warning
was to see a herd of buffalo being pursued
by hunters on horseback. And then there were
certain signs that were helpful: A flock, or
even two or three crows flying straight
toward us when we were traveling meant that
enemies were somewhere near by. Wind
blowing straight upon us, down upon the grass

and the ground, and then straight up, was also a sign that enemies were not far off.

'One summer, when we Blood People were encamped on Belly River, Pikû´ni friends of mine, Bird Rattle, Short Man, and Lone Rider, came from the south to visit me, and after a time we decided to go to war. As my woman, as usual, accompanied me, we were a party of five.

'We were quite tired when we arrived at Aiya Kî´mîkwi [Hills-on-Both-Sides; Cypress Hills] early one morning, so we rested there that day and all the following night. During the night I had a strange vision: Came to me a very old man, and said: "You are to see a coyote. Watch the animal, notice the direction that his nose is pointing, and go you that way, and you will find horses." Having said that, the old man vanished.

'When we awoke, in the morning, I told my companions of my vision, and they thought, as I did, that it was without value. But while we were eating some meat that we had broiled, a coyote appeared upon a rise of ground quite near us, and, looking straight to the south, never once at us, it raised its quavering yelp. Four times it did that — four, the sacred number — and then trotted off southward and out of our sight. And said Bird Rattle to me: "I was mistaken about your vision. It meant something of value to us. Your vision animal looked straight to the south all the time it was near us. So is it that we must go south, instead of east-and-south to Little River, as we intended."

'We were all agreed that this was the thing for us to do. My woman asked: "Do we remain here until night, and then go on?" We were afoot, and so traveling only in the night-time, for it was very dangerous for small parties afoot to travel in the daytime, likely as they would be to be discovered by a large party of enemies traveling through the country.

" 'I think that we should go on as soon as we finish eating," I replied.

' "No. Too dangerous," said my woman.

' "Not so. His vision was that we are to find horses by going in the direction to which the coyote's nose pointed; therefore it must be that by the vision Old Man meant for us to travel in daytime; for, were we to travel only at night, we could not see horses unless we should happen to walk right to them."

'That was the opinion of the others of the party. We finished eating, took up our weapons and other belongings, and went on south across the plain, and in the middle of the day discovered five horses a little way ahead of us. But they were wild horses; no sooner did they see us than they raised their tails and ran, never stopped running so long as they were in sight. We wondered if they were the horses of my vision.

'We went on and on, and near night discovered a few riders well to the south of us, and going south, down the valley of Little River, in which was probably their camp. When night came, we went on, and, upon arriving at the rim of the river valley, looked down upon a camp of more than a hundred lodges; lodges of our enemy, the Assiniboins, right there in our own country. Well they knew that our Blood tribe and the Blackfeet were far to the north, and the Pikû'ni far west, at the foot of the Backbone [the Rocky Mountains], or they would never have dared to camp where they were.

'And now was my vision truly fulfilled, for down in the valley were many bands of horses; hundreds and hundreds of horses; some of them well out from the camp and quite near us. We went down among them, and with the ropes that we carried, caught each of us one and I another one for my woman. We mounted them and surrounded and drove off northward a fine band of the animals, and without alarming their owners. We were happy. As soon as we were well out upon the plain, we sang song after song;

victory songs; songs of war. It was a night when Old Woman [the moon] was showing all of herself, above us in the blue. So was it that we were enabled to count our takings; including those that we rode, they were forty-four big strong horses.

'At midnight, we turned west, again struck Little River, then turned up it, northward again, or somewhat west of north, and at daylight, being very tired, we stopped to rest at the foot of a very steep little butte not far east of the East Butte of the Sweetgrass Three Buttes. Haiya! Just as my woman was starting a fire of some dry willows that she had gathered, there came charging at us a large party of Cree riders, some of them coming down the valley, the others up it. We were surrounded; we could not possibly mount our horses and escape from them. There was but one thing for us to do, and we did it: we ran to the top of the steep butte, threw up a circle of the large rocks that were there plentiful, and lay down within it.

'Shouting their weak Cree war cry, the enemy came charging up that steep hill, thinking to overcome us easily. We fired at them with careful aim, wounded one of them, and killed two of the horses that they rode. Back down the hill they went, faster than they had come up it. We expected them to come again, and, when they showed no intention to do so, I went out to where I could look down upon them, and dared them to come and try to kill us. They did not answer me; they did not even fire at me: they rounded up the horses that we had taken and drove them off northeast. We were again afoot.

'Said my woman to me: "Just nothing, that vision of yours. What good did it do us? None."

'Said Bird Rattle to her: "Woman, be careful. It is not safe to speak ill of our visions. You may bring great trouble upon us by doing so. So far as your man's vision went, it was good. As it foretold, we did find horses, we captured horses. That, doubtless, was as far as the old man of the vision had knowledge of the future. He could not have known that the horses would be taken from us."

" 'All I will say, then, is that we are again afoot and I think that we should go home," she answered.

" 'I am not going home," I said. "I started out to get the enemy horses and I am going to have them. From here I am going to our friends, the Entrails People [Gros Ventres], for a short visit with them, and then on to raid the Sioux or some other enemy."

" 'Good! I am with you," said Bird Rattle. The others said the same. Came night, and we struck out for the Bear Paw Mountains, where, as we had learned before leaving Belly River, the Entrails People were encamped; on the east side of them, on a little fork of Middle Creek. [Calf Creek, putting into the Missouri at Cow Island.] We were five nights on our way to the creek, and when we arrived there, we found that the tribe had broken camp and gone north, probably out to Little River. We went into the timber, rested, broiled and ate some meat of an antelope that we had killed, slept, and, soon after sunset, struck off north, expecting to strike the camp of our friends soon after daylight. We did not follow their trail, as it was winding this way and that way between the hills, and so did not learn that, having gone over the ridge between the Bear Paw and the Wolf Mountains, they had turned west and were, as we later learned, encamped on Sand Creek. Yes. Our big mistake was in making a straight course to Little River, instead of following their trail. Sun was well up when we sighted the valley of the river, saw the smoke of a big camp rising from it, saw some riders coming out to hunt.

'One of the riders discovered us, came to us, and who should he be but a one-time member of our own tribe, a man named Sliding Down. Many winters before, he had captured an

Assiniboin woman, and soon had so loved her that he would do anything that she asked of him. She had persuaded him to go with her to live with her tribe, and since then he had visited us but twice.

'Now, as soon as we recognized this rider, we knew that it was an enemy camp, a camp of the Assiniboins, there ahead of us in the valley, and so we felt we were in great danger. Sliding Down was pleased when he found that we were from his own tribe, and said that we must accompany him to his camp and make him a long visit. I replied that the one thing for us to do was to turn back the way we had come, for to enter the camp of our worst enemies would result in but one thing, death for us all. He pointed to the riders here and there upon the plain, several of them coming toward us, and said that it was too late for us to retreat; that we must accompany him to camp, and right to the chief's lodge, where he would talk for us, and we would be safe.

'He was right; our one chance to live was to do as he urged. There was no place upon that level plain to which we could retreat and fight with any chance of success. We moved on toward the camp, Sliding Down riding beside us. The people saw us coming, gathered together and stared at us, saw that we were

Bloods and Pikû´ni, and made great outcry, without doubt calling us bad names and saying that we must be killed.

'The chief of this band of the Assiniboins was Big Belly Boy. Sliding Down led us straight to his lodge and into it. The chief, sitting upon his couch, looked up at us, but did not invite us to take seats; said nothing. We sat down anyhow, all of us in a row upon the couches on the left side of the lodge. Sliding Down talked to the chief, and he said but little in reply, and that little very angrily. I could see that Sliding Down was worried; terribly uneasy.

'After a time he said to us: "The chief says that his leading men are all out hunting; that when they return he will talk with them, and decide what to do with you."

' "Meaning that we are to be killed," I said.
' "No! No! They shall not do that. I will talk for you, so take courage," he replied.

'So there we sat. We were given neither a smoke, a drink of water, nor food, which in itself meant that we were to be killed. The day seemed to be endless. There we sat all through it, constantly on watch, with ever-ready rifles, and outside, surrounding the lodge, a crowd calling us bad names, threatening us with death, a crowd that never lessened. Now and then the chief filled his pipe and smoked, all by himself. He once went out and was gone for some time; doubtless to eat in some other lodge. It was night when the men he had called upon came into the lodge and sat down. His women then raised the lodge skin all around the lodge, and the crowd surrounding it stared in at us.

'Suddenly the chief pointed a finger to me, said, and signed to me: "You are a bad man. You are crazy to come into my camp without invitation to come."

' "You are a liar," I signed back. "I am not crazy. I did not come here without invitation. My friend, Sliding Down, once of my tribe, now one of your tribe, invited me, and those with me, to come here. Yes, you are a liar."

'No sooner had I said that than the chief drew out his big knife and started to rise from his seat to come at me. But before he could straighten up, I was upon my feet, as were my companions, rifles cocked, ready to shoot, my woman also ready with her six-shooter. And as I rose up, I roared; very loudly roared, just as an angry grizzly roars. I kept on roaring, champing my jaws; glaring at the chief and his men. I frightened them terribly. Sliding Down shouted something to them, and they fled from the lodge, out through the doorway and out under the raised lodge skin; all of them but the chief, his woman, and Sliding Down. The chief was again sitting upon his couch, his woman beside him. He laid his knife upon the ground; he bent over, head drooping as though he was very tired. Sliding Down signed to me that he — the chief — was through with us. I knew it. I told my people to leave the lodge, and they went out one by one while I stood pointing my cocked rifle at the chief. Then I went out; went out backward, rifle pointed at the chief until I could no longer see him. There was now no crowd of people around the lodge; not a man, woman, or child was in sight; all had fled, for, as I long afterward learned from Sliding Down, he had shouted, there in the lodge, that I was very dangerous, very powerful; that Sun was strongly with me. So was it that we were not fired at nor followed as we went out of the camp and up the river valley.

'Two nights of travel from that enemy camp, and we arrived in the camp of our friends, the Entrails People, on Sand Creek. We told them of our narrow escape from the Assiniboins, and asked them how it was that they allowed them to camp and hunt in our country. They replied that they did not feel that they were strong enough to attack and drive them east to their own country. It was the duty of us Blood People, the Blackfeet, and the Pikû´ni, to aid them in keeping the Assiniboins where they belonged, east of the mouth of Little River.

'As I have said, Bird Rattle, Short Man and Lone Rider, my companions, were members of the Pikû'ni tribe of us Plains People. Said Bird Rattle now: "You Entrails People, do not put the blame for this upon my tribe. They do not know that the Assiniboins are here in our country, killing our buffalo and other food animals. It was for you to send word to them about it, but you didn't. Well, I am going to them, going to bring them here, and together we will make those Cut-Throats cry. All I ask of you now is a horse, that I may quickly do this."

" 'And a horse for me, too. I will go with him to our people," said Short Man.

'Every Entrails man there present offered a horse. My friends took the first two that were brought in, and rode off to the west to find their tribe. They did find them; brought them to the Bear Paws, and, with the Entrails People, they attacked the Assiniboins, made a great killing of them, and drove the survivors back into their own country. But I was not there to take part in it.

'After a rest of two nights in the camp of the Entrails People, Lone Rider, my wife, and I, started south to raid the Crows. Our friends in the big camp offered us horses, but we preferred to go on foot.

'Arriving at Big River [the Missouri River], we made a raft of driftwood and safely crossed it, and in the timber on the south side, I shot a buffalo and wounded another with my bow and arrows, which I always carried in order to get meat without noise. Leaving my woman and Lone Rider to take the tongue and a little of the meat of my kill, I went on after the wounded one, and, just as I killed it, my woman overtook me and said that she had seen a man up on the rim of the valley. I looked up at it from the edge of the grove. It was strewn with huge rocks, sparsely grown with small pines. I could see no man, and told her that she must have mistaken one of the pines for a man, but she insisted that she had seen a man there, walking, with a gun upon his shoulder. In the shelter of a deep and narrow coulee, and then thick brush of the slope, I went up onto the rim, my woman following, and, hearing some one coming our way, singing a low, strange song, we crouched down in the shelter of a big rock surrounded with thick juniper brush. The man came on, still singing his low song, a Crow he was, and was passing close in front of us, when, with my loud, like-a-mad-grizzly-bear roaring, I sprang out at him, frightening him so badly that he dropped his gun; and, seeing me with my rifle pointed at him, he dared not pick it up nor run. Instead, he held his hands out toward me, and, crying, signed to me to pity him. Yes, he bellowed shrilly; tears rolled down his cheeks. My woman said to me: "Move over! Let me kill him!" She cocked her six-shooter, and started to aim it at him; but I felt sudden and great pity for the man because he was crying. I told her that she should not kill him; told the man, signed to him, that I gave him his life. I took up his rifle. Lone Rider joined us, and I talked with my captive, in the sign language, of course. He said that he was a Crow — as I well knew by the way his hair was dressed. He had lost his woman. When she died, he had felt so badly that he had left his people and was just wandering about by himself and mourning for her. He was now thinking that he would go on down the river and visit the Entrails People of the Earth Houses, some of whom were his relatives.[1] I handed him his rifle, and told him to go. He turned and left us, went down the slope of the valley, never once looking back at us. Then my woman and Lone Rider scolded me; said that I should not have given the man, a Crow, one of our

[1] The Hidatsa — Minnetarees.

193

worst enemies, his life. I told them that I had so pitied him that I could not kill him. I raised my hands to Sun and asked him to pity me; to give me success in my undertakings; to be good to me even as I had pitied this my enemy and given him his life.

'(Here is a strange happening. Three summers back, when I was visiting the Pikû´ni, this Crow came from his Bighorn River country, came in the fire wagons, also to visit them, and we met, recognized one another, though we were now both of us old and wrinkled and gray-haired. His name was Bear Snake. Said he: "Sun heard you, yes, Above One heard you when you had pity for me, and has let us meet. Yes, here we are together, talking to one another. It is good.")

'Traveling by night, well cached and resting by day, we three at last crossed Elk River, ascended Bighorn River, and at daylight, one morning, looked down upon a big camp of the Crows, and their many bands of horses grazing around it. We hid in a thick growth of cherry brush on a slope of the valley, slept by turns, ate some dried meat that we had, watched the Crows go out to hunt, and saw them return, their horses loaded with buffalo meat. Came night, and we went down into the valley, approached the camp, sat down near it until the singing, dancing, visiting, and feasting of the people ceased, and they slept. Lone Rider and I then went into the camp and led out horses that were tied close to their owners, their war horses, their fast buffalo horses, and brought them to my woman to hold while we went in for more of them. It is very dangerous, that taking of horses out of an enemy camp. Each time we went in for them, we went well knowing that we might not come out alive. At any time we were likely to be discovered and shot down. The second time we went in, as we were approaching a lodge to which two big gray horses were tied, their ropes secured to the pegs of the lodge skin, we heard a deep, heavy cough within it, and stopped and lay down flat at the edge of a not high growth of sagebrush. And just in time, for a man came out of the lodge, stood staring this way and that way, went to the two horses, examined their ropes, and then went back into the lodge. We lay right where we were for some time, then went to another part of the camp; heard heavy snoring in a lodge near which three horses were tied; we took them. Five times we entered the camp, and took out altogether fourteen horses. Then mounting three of them, we started down the valley, I in the lead, my woman and Lone Rider driving the loose

horses close after me. We went slowly until out of
sight and hearing of the camp, then swiftly, as fast
as we possibly could, and at daybreak came to Elk
River [the Yellowstone] and without trouble swam
it with our takings. We went on and on all that
long day, with but one short rest. No doubt the
Crows found and took our trail, but we had the
best of them: frequent changes of horses. So was
it that we never saw them. Some days later, we
rode into the camp of our people, on Belly River,
singing a victory song. So ended that raid against
the enemy.'

CHAPTER IX

LEANING-OVER-BUTCHERING

ITOKIN´ INO´TA (Leaning-Over-Butchering) is the only surviving one of the old-time great warriors of his tribe, the North Pikû´ni, and is now seventy-four years of age. We found the tales that he told us, during our encampment at Waterton Lake, very interesting. Put together they were as follows :

'Although I went to war twenty-seven times, I was never wounded. I attribute my whole skin to the protection of feathered-legged hawk, who came to me when, in my seventeenth winter, I went up onto Chief Mountain and there fasted and prayed for a sacred helper. As I slept, this swift flier, so swift and sure that it seizes and kills flying ducks, came to me and promised that it would pity me, help me in all of my undertakings. So surely and powerfully did it help me, strengthen my prayers to Sun, that, more than once I escaped from attacks of the enemy that seemed impossible for me to survive. But though never even wounded, I was not always successful in my raids. Upon more than one of them I lost close friends who were with me, and suffered terribly, as in this one of which I will tell you, the worst one of all.

'We were encamped on Ka'iyîs Isak'ta [Dried Meat River; Musselshell River], near its confluence with Big River [the Missouri]. Our tribe had been on the south of Big River all winter; in the midst of so many herds of buffalo that they blackened the plains. We had traded in our many well-tanned buffalo robes, our winter take of furs, at Many Houses [Fort Benton], and now, as the gooseberries were beginning to ripen, here we were on Ka'iyîs Isak'ta, and some of us were eager to go to war. We made up a party of fourteen, under the leadership of a man named Low Horn, and started out on foot to seek the camp of the Crows, and raid it.

'We left camp when Sun was in the middle, and stopped for the night on Crooked Creek. Came day, and, while we were broiling and eating some antelope meat, our leader told us that he had had a dream, and could not understand its meaning, whether for good or for trouble for us ahead.

He had seen a number of enemies on horseback, charging in upon us, their leader a big, wide-shouldered man, wearing a beautiful, long-tailed headdress of eagle tail feathers. Well, what did we think it meant?

'We considered it earnestly. I alone replied that I believed it a bad luck dream; a warning to us to turn back, to return to our people. But all the others were agreed that it was a good luck dream; that it foretold we were to meet the enemy and make a killing of them. So was it that, against my advice, we went on.

'That evening we made camp near Black Butte, and I had a dream; I heard a woman crying out to us, "I have pity for you." I looked all around, could not see a woman anywhere. I said to my companions: "Did you hear that? Was it a woman ?"

'One and all, they answered: "I don't know. I heard nothing."

'I then heard loud and strange war cries, and again looked all around, but nowhere were any enemies in sight. And I said to my companions: "Did you hear that, war cries of an enemy party?"

'As before, they answered, each one of them, "I heard nothing."

'Just before daylight I awoke, awakened my companions, told them my dream, and that I believed it a bad luck dream, a warning to us to turn back.

'They laughed. The leader, Low Horn, said to me: "If you feel that way about it, you can go back. We are going on."

'I went on with them, but with low heart, not happily, eagerly, as I had felt upon my previous war trails. I had another reason for uneasiness. After I had told my companions my dream, when day came, we looked out upon the plain stretching away north to the breaks of Big River, and eastward to Dried Meat River, and saw that the herds of buffalo upon it were disturbed; traveling this way and that way; bunching up and looking this way and that way, and again moving on. Yet we could see no reason for it; nowhere were there men in sight, men on horseback or afoot. I prayed to my sacred helper; prayed Sun to pity me, to keep me safe from the dangers ahead of us.

'We were going south now, on our right the Snow Mountains, on our left the valley of Dried Meat River. Near the end of the day we neared a small creek, Sand Creek, that runs into it. Red Old Man, Running Coyote, and I were well in the lead, Low Horn having sent us on to scout for our party. We were traveling through a long stretch of quaking aspens upon the slope of the mountain. Below us was a wide grassy flat, and at the foot of it the creek. My companions proposed to go to it to drink.

"Don't go down there in the open, where enemies may discover you," I said. "Let us go on through these quaking aspens to the top of that ridge, from which we can see a long way in every direction. Then, if it seems to be safe, you can go down and drink."

'But they would not listen; they were very thirsty; they were going for water at once. They left me, and, when they were nearing the creek, six riders appeared on that ridge, enemies, of course, and I ran down to help them fight, and they ran up toward me, and we met in the center of the open slope. The riders had stopped. Their leader, on a big, white horse, dismounted, and the others did, too. The leader signed to us: "Stand where you are." And then, "Who are you?"

' "Pikûní," I signed. "Come and fight us." I signed that because I knew that the rest of our party could not be far behind, and that, together, we could easily kill the six riders. But their leader signed to us:"You go back whence you came." He then draped his black blanket upon his rifle and twirled it around him four times, meaning, "We are four camps of people."

"Who are you?" I signed. But he did not answer. We saw, just then, our leader and other companions running through the quaking aspens to get to the summit of the ridge and attack the enemy, and we ran toward them, too. I doubt that they saw our companions, but they must have suspected that we were but three of a large party, and that they were in danger, for they mounted their horses and disappeared, and, when we all arrived upon the summit of the ridge, they were nowhere in sight. Then our leader, learning that we all could have easily ambuscaded the six, had it not been for Red Old Man's and Running Coyote's great mistake in exposing themselves in order to get a drink, scolded them severely, and was angry at me for allowing them to go out into the open. I could have replied that I urged them not to go down to the creek, but said nothing.

'We passed the night in a grove of cottonwoods and willows bordering Sand Creek. The next morning, keeping always in the timber and brush, we followed Sand Creek down to its junction with Dried Meat Creek, and then turned up its timbered valley. White Antelope and I were the scouts for our party, and well in the lead. We were following a well-worn buffalo trail, smooth and hard. I was a few steps ahead of my companion, when he called to me to stop, and, pointing to something at the side of the trail, said, "See what I have found." It was a small image of a human being; a soft-rock carving. Its face was painted yellow and its right leg had been broken off below the knee, and that part of it was missing. Its right hand was pressed against its breast, its left arm and hand straight down against its side. White Antelope took it up, kissed it, handed it to me, and said that it had probably been made for a child; a child's plaything. I did not think so. I believed it to be a sacred object, and, because of its broken and missing leg, a bad omen for us. I looked it over carefully, and then set it upon a rock at the side of the trail just as our leader and the others of our party came up. They looked at it, made fun of it, and Red Old Man threw a stone at it and broke its left leg and left arm. I picked it up, took it away from the trail a little way, prayed to it to pity me, to aid me in surviving the danger which I felt was upon us. I then hid it under a fallen tree, with a gift that I made it, a bear claw that I took from my necklace, and rejoined my party.

'During that day of travel up the valley, we crossed and recrossed the creek, looking for signs of the enemy, but found not even a horse track. We stopped for the night in a growth of willows close to the creek, and near morning I had a dream; a man whom I could not see, said loudly, again and again, "Well, if you will not listen to me—"

'I told my companions my dream, and that I believed it another omen of bad luck for us. Some of them laughed, and said that I was always looking for unlucky signs. Our leader looked very solemn, very thoughtful, and after a time said to us: "To-day after Sun has passed the middle of the blue, if we see no signs of the enemy, you young ones will put up a sweat lodge for us old ones. The time has come for us to do some praying; to make some sacrifices to the Powerful One Above."

'We ate the last of our meat, that morning. We moved on up the valley, and, as on the day before, could find no least sign of the enemy. When Sun was in the middle, our leader called a halt and a rest, and told two of our bow-and-arrows men — there were only six guns in our party — to kill some meat for us. They were gone some time, returned with the meat of a buffalo calf, and said that they had also shot its mother. She fell, lay as though she were dead, and, going to her, they cut her hide from her head down the back to the tail, so that they could easily get at the dorsal ribs and loin meat that they wanted. But they didn't get it; to their great surprise, she suddenly sprang up and ran off, kept on running so long as she was in sight. Strange, was it not? they asked, and was it not a bad luck sign?

'None answered them. We all knew that it was a very bad sign. Said our leader: "Let us move on and find a suitable place for our sweat lodge."

'We went on and on; saw many places that were suitable for a sweat lodge, willows just right for its frame, the creek near by, but one or another of our elders made objections to each one of them, and said that there must be a better place farther on. And at last, the day was so far gone that our leader said we would have to defer to the next day the making of it. Another bad omen.

'Sun was setting when we saw, close ahead, that the valley made a sudden sharp bend to the right, and to save time and distance we started to cut across the point of the treeless, brushless but grassy ridge that formed the bend. We had, somehow, separated into two groups to cross it, one of eight, the other of six men. I was one of the six, and we were quite a long way to the right of the eight. We saw that a narrow coulee ran down the center of the ridge, and that, at the head of it, there was a very large grove of quaking aspens. As we neared the coulee, many enemy riders suddenly came charging from the creek, the valley, up each side of it, and we, as well as the eight below us, and both parties of us ran to the coulee and jumped down into it, there to defend ourselves as best we could. Where we six were, the coulee, though narrow, was not deep; its banks were just about level with our heads as we stood in it. A poor place for us to be. I said to my companions: "I wish that we had gone to the quaking aspen grove above; we must try to go there." And then I prayed: "O Sun! O sacred bird! Save us. If you have no pity, then soon our bodies will be lying here, swelling horribly," I said.

'There must have been all of a hundred of the enemy. Already some of them were attacking our companions below, the others coming on toward us six, shouting their war cries. "We are in a terrible trap. The many bad omens that we have had since we started out upon this trail, this is what they meant," I said to our leader, Low Horn, standing at my side.

'Don't fear. We are all right," he answered, and I thought that he must be crazy.

'All right?" I asked. "Ha! My father, a chief, my mother and relatives, are going to lose me this day."

'And then the riders were close on both sides of us, shooting down at us, circling away and coming around to shoot again. The smoke of their guns and of ours was a thick dark cloud above us. Through it I saw a dismounted enemy dimly; red-shirted, striped black-and-white painted face, raising his gun to shoot at us, and I shot him; shot him in his breast, saw him fall. I heard a bullet thud into Red Old Man, at my side. He fell and died. And right after that Low Horn, close on my left, was killed; then another, Mud Head. There remained only Running Coyote, White Antelope, and I. Of all our party, I was the best armed. I had a many-shots rifle, one of the first of them that the Big Knives traders brought to our country in their fireboats, and, when this fight began, I had in two belts more than a hundred cartridges for it.[1] I said now to the two: "My friends, for us to remain here is to die. Our one chance to survive is to get

---

[1] An 1866 model, .44 caliber, Henry repeating rifle. The American Fur Company's successor, Carroll & Steell, sold several cases of them to the Blackfeet tribes, at Fort Benton, Montana, in 1867.

into that big quaking aspen grove up there. Let us try it. But, first, we must try to drive away those who are fighting us."

'Go! We are with you," Running Coyote replied.

'We climbed the left bank of the coulee, and when out of it, saw that the greater number of our enemies — they proved to be Sioux — were still fighting the eight of our party, or those of them still alive, in the lower part of the coulee. There were thirty or forty in the attack upon us, about half of them on our side of the coulee and half on its other side. I fired five or six shots at those across, fired as fast as I could work the lever of my rifle and aim it, then turned and fired at the others, just then turning to ride close past us again. Their leader, on a big roan horse, was a heavy-bodied man, wearing a white shirt dotted with red paint, and a black blanket. I took good aim at him, fired, and he threw up his hands, dropped his gun, swayed forth and back, and dropped sideways from his horse. At the same time, Running Coyote broke a leg of another rider, the bullet going on into his horse and killing it. I was shooting so fast that the rest of the riders wheeled off from us instead of coming close in, as they had intended. I turned again and fired a number of shots at those across from us, and they, too, drew off, to fire at us from a safer distance; and at that we started for the grove above. Bullets whistled past us; struck the ground around us. I made a vow to Sun: "Even though I am surrounded by the enemy, I am going to give you a lodge," I said.

'Soon after that, a bullet struck Running Coyote, tore into his left side; blood gushed from his mouth and nose, and he fell and died. White Antelope and I went on, he loading and firing his muzzle-loader now and then, I shooting as fast as I could fill the magazine of my rifle with cartridges, and then lever them into the barrel; and always I tried to fire with careful aim. So was it that we could not make very swift progress toward the grove. We had to keep shooting at our enemies in order to prevent them from closing in on us. I saw that they feared my many-shots rifle; it was, perhaps, the first one of that kind that they had ever seen.

'At last we neared the grove. Sun had set, the evening was already dusk, and, though the enemy bullets were striking all around us, I had hope that we were to survive. And then, when we were no more than a hundred steps from the edge of the grove, that hope suddenly died. An enemy bullet struck White Antelope and he fell, cried out to me: "My friend, my friend, do not leave me."

'With you to the end," I answered. I thought that he was soon to die. But the bullet had only torn the muscles of his left leg above the knee. He got up, and, using his gun as a cane, limped slowly on, I following and shooting at the enemy. We neared the grove slowly, but nearer and nearer, and again I had hope that we were to reach its shelter, and so escape the enemy. But when we were not fifty steps from it, my friend was shot again; the bullet pierced his lungs, probably his heart also; he dropped to the ground and with a gasp or two was dead. Well, I had kept my promise; I had stayed with him to his end. But now I ran; ran swiftly into the grove and stopped and looked back. The enemies, who had been shooting at my companions and me, did not dare to come on to count *coup* upon the body of White Antelope, for they knew that, from my hiding-place in the grove, I could kill many of them. Instead, they raised their victory song and rode swiftly down to count *coups* upon Running Coyote, and then the others in the coulee below him. And still farther down, the greater number of the enemy were singing and counting *coups* upon the eight of our party who had there been wiped out. Was I sad? I mourned for my companions, all dead, all scalped, mutilated, save White Antelope, was so sorrowful that I became sick; my legs would not support me. I dropped to the ground and lay there for a long time.

'When, at last, I felt able to travel, Night-Light was well up in the sky. I counted my remaining cartridges; seven in the magazine of my rifle, six in one of my belts. I had fired at the enemy more than a hundred times, and, so far as I knew, had killed but two of them; small, small pay for all that they had done to us. I scolded myself. Why hadn't I fired with more careful aim? I knew the answer; I had been too excited, too frightened to do that, to make every shot count. I hated myself. I got upon my feet, went and looked out from the edge of the grove. None of the enemy was in sight, but away up the valley I could see tree-tops bright with the light of fire under them, and hear singing and the beating of drums: the enemy were there, dancing with the scalps, the long hair that I had so often seen my companions neatly comb and braid, and end-tie with narrow strips of sacred otter fur. I went northward through the grove, on into the valley of Dried Meat Creek, and on down it until break of day, when I hid in some willows beside the stream. I was very hungry, but had no meat, and dared not risk killing any.

'Mourning over the death of my friends, I slept but little during the day. As soon as it was dark, I went on again, but slowly, weakly, from lack of food. One of my moccasins was ripping and I had no needle, sinew thread, or awl to re-sew it; they were in my war sack that I had dropped when we were in the coulee, fighting the enemy. And now, as I was working my way through a grove, the sole of the moccasin was ripped completely off by a projecting stick. I went on still more slowly, painfully, wearing my one good moccasin first on one foot, then on the other. Day came. I was a long way from where my dead and mutilated companions lay. I had to have meat. Though the Sioux might be near by in the valley, looking for me, I must take the risk and shoot a buffalo or antelope, elk or deer, whichever of them would first appear. Buffalo were the first, a small band of them coming to the creek for water. As they were passing me, I fired through the brush at a yearling; never touched it; the bullet must have struck a twig and glanced another way, I thought. I levered another cartridge from the magazine, but could not force it into the barrel. I examined it, saw that I was done for: the base of the cartridge that I had fired had blown off, the remainder of it was fast in the barrel, and there would remain until I could get an awl with which to pry it loose. Then was my heart truly low, my body weak. I sat down under the trees; then dropped flat upon the ground, and became as one dead.

'It was late in the day when I came to life again. I staggered to the creek and drank, then went slowly, weakly, down the valley in a smooth buffalo trail. More and more slowly as my hunger, my need of food increased. And I was powerless to obtain any, my rifle of no more use to me than a stick. I prayed to my sacred helper, and then to Sun: "Pity me! Help me to return to my people; later to build the sacred lodge that I promised you," I said. And I thought about the vision I had had while lying as though dead. Passed before me my thirteen companions, in single file, Low Horn in the lead. But they were not real; they were just the shadows of their persons; I could see through them. They passed slowly by me, sad of face, looking neither to the right nor left. I had hoped that some of them had escaped from the attack upon us, but now I knew that I alone survived. But to what end? Without food, I could never get back to the camp of my people.

'Ha! Not useless my prayers. Staggering along that trail, I found quite near it the remains of a buffalo that had been killed by human beings, probably by a war party; for it had been skinned, and the hide thrown aside, and the wolves had pretty well cleaned the bones of the meat that the killers had left upon them. Still, there were the leg bones, full of marrow, and a few strips of meat adhering to the hide. I cut off the strips, took the larger bones, and went back into the timber with them, built a little fire, and soon was eating broiled meat and marrow. A little; not all that I wanted, lest I should become sick. And almost at once my strength came back to me. I gathered up the remainder of the bones and meat that I had roasted, got more from the remains of the buffalo, cut a lot of hair from the head of the hide, with which to bind my moccasinless foot, and went on. And so, three days later, was once more with my people. Ha! What mourning, what sadness of widows and orphans there was in that camp when I had told that, of our party of fourteen, I alone survived!'

As Leaning-Over-Butchering never was able to touch the two Sioux that he killed in this fight nor take their weapons, he was not entitled to number them with his *coups*. The *coups* that he does rightly count are as follows:

Enemies killed, struck, and weapons taken: Three Crows; five Assiniboins; four Crees; one Pend d'Oreille.

Horse *coups*, ten; taken in battle with enemies, and from enemy camps, in all, more than three hundred head.

Enemy lives spared, two.

More than once, during the talks around our lodge fires, Leaning-Over-Butchering spoke of the latter two *coups*. Said he:

'It may be, I think it likely, that my success,' my safety in war, was partly due to the real pity that I had for those two enemies. The first one of them was a Snake man. I was the leader of a war party against the Crows. Upon our way south, at Yellow River [Judith River], we discovered a one-lodge camp; a small, tattered, smoke-stained lodge. Sitting in front of it were a man and two women. Near them were five small poor horses. I told my men to remain where they were; that I would go alone against this enemy. As I cautiously worked my way through the timber and brush, the women went into the lodge and remained there. The man sat cross-legged upon the ground, head down, arms folded across his breast. At his side lay his bow and arrows, in a worn old case of fur. He did not see nor hear me until, standing a few steps in front of him and with half-raised rifle, I suddenly said, "Hai!" He flinched; looked up at me. I thought that I had never seen a face so thin and worn; eyes so big and sad. He raised trembling hands to me; said something in his strange language; tears rolled down his cheeks; he signed to me to pity him. I did pity him. I could not help it: "Be not afraid," I signed. "I shall not strike you."

'His women came out of the lodge and saw me sign that to him. As they hurried to him, my men came running in, shouting to me: "Stand aside! We will kill them!"

'I sprang in front of the three, motioned my men to stop, to stand; told them that there were to be no killings; that I had great pity for the poor ones. My men did not like that; they urged me to let them kill the three. I replied that they need talk no more about it, for I had given the three their lives. So was it that we had a short visit with the man, and he told us that he was a Snake man. He was trying to find the camp of his people, from whom he had separated on the other side of the Backbone [Rocky Mountains] some moons back; and three days back, his son, a good hunter, had been killed by a big bear. We had, amongst us, quite a lot of meat that we had killed, even some pemmican that our women had given us for our long trail. I told my men to give it all to the poor ones. They did so and we went upon our way. Yes, and ten nights later, on Big Horn River, we rounded up more than a hundred Crow horses, and, though pursued, got safely away with them.

'And now the other one to whom I gave his life: We were camped on Rope-Stretched-Across Creek [Lee's Creek], right where is now the town of the Many-Wives white men [Mormons]. And, though we did not know it, right here at this lake the whole tribe of the Kûtenai were in camp. Late one evening, several of our young hunters returned to camp and reported a very large herd of buffalo, up in the valley of Belly River. Early the next morning, more than forty of us mounted our swiftest horses and started out to run the herd. We saw it from afar; hundreds and hundreds of the buffalo, upon the plain to the north of the river, but still close to the rim of the valley. We went down into the valley and up it until opposite the herd, then made ready to go up the slope and charge right into the herd. But when we topped the rim, what was our surprise when we saw other riders charging right into it; thirty or more of them; enemies; Kûtenai men, as we knew by their dress, the fashion of their hair. So was it that we charged them, instead of the buffalo. They scattered to the north, the west, the south. I went after one who was riding a yellow horse; a fast horse, but my buffalo runner was just a little faster. Slowly I gained upon the man, saw that he had bow and arrows, but no gun. I said to myself: "I will count a real *coup* upon this enemy: I will ride up beside him, and strike him with my whip before killing him."

'Not until I was almost up with him did he make any move at me. Then, as he turned and attempted to fire an arrow at me, I struck at his bow with my rifle, and the end of the barrel caught in its lower end, where the string was tied to it, and swept it out of his grip. It fell to the ground, the arrow, too, and he then whipped and heeled his horse, trying to make it go faster. He was wearing a deer-leather shirt. I reached out, grasped the neck of it, and gave a hard, quick yank, and, as the man slipped from his horse, he reached out and tried to seize me and take me to the ground with him. He failed to get a firm grip and struck the ground with head and shoulder, but by the time I slowed my horse and turned back toward him, he was upon his feet, hands at ease, watching me as if he did not care what I might do. Then, when I rode quite near him and checked my horse, he signed: "Don't sit up there staring at me. Let us be done with it; shoot me."

'Ha! That Kûtenai was so brave, so much a brave, a real man, that I could not kill him. "No. I shall not kill you," I signed. I raised my hand to Sun and to him said and signed: "Sky Chief, I give this Kûtenai his life. You see. You see me that I do not even strike him. Have pity on me."

'And then I said to the man: "Go take up your bow; catch your horse; go whither you will, I am through with you."

" 'Your heart is good; you are generous. In some future day we may meet again. If we can meet as friends, I shall be glad," he signed.

'Yes. That will be good," I answered.

'As I rode away, and after a time looked back, he was upon his horse and going toward the mountains. Long afterwards, when we at last made peace with the Kûtenai People, I did meet the man, Fisher Running, and we became good friends.

'You ask what of his companions, that day? My fellow hunters killed four of them. The others, returned to their camp here, told that they had been discovered and set upon by us Bloods, and the tribe packed up their belongings and headed for their country on the other side of the Backbone, and for a long time did not return to steal more of our buffalo.

'Kyi! I have finished.'

CHAPTER X

EAGLE PLUME

A MOST likable man is our friend, Pi´ta Sahpwopi (Eagle Plume), a chief of the Ka´ina (Blood) tribe of the Blackfeet Confederacy. He is one of the few of them now living who has any great war record. His *coups* include twenty-two expeditions against enemy tribes, in which he killed in all seven men, and secured more than a hundred enemy horses. His story of what he considers his most successful raid is as follows:

'One beginning-of-summer-time, when we Ka´ina were encamped on Belly River, close up to the Backbone, I called upon nine men, good warriors all of them, to go with me upon a raid south; a raid upon the Crows. Before leaving, we built a sweat lodge of good size, and asked Three Bears, owner of the Beaver Medicine Roll, to join us in it, and pray for our success and safe return. He was very glad to do that, and, after we left for the south, he mounted a horse, near going down of Sun of every day, and rode all through the camp, shouting the name of each member of our party, and calling upon the people to pray for us. That in itself is a powerful aid to a war party. It sustains them, gives them courage. Each evening they think, they say to one another: "Right now, our Sun priest is riding about in camp, praying for us, asking the people to pray for us. It is good, it is powerful. We must deserve their prayers."

'Many youths wanted to go with us, to wait upon us, and so learn the ways of the warrior. I selected one of them, a good hunter, a good shot, a youth named Wolf Plume. He carried my Thunder Medicine Pipe, my shield, my ropes. When we made camp, and I went off by myself to rest, to sleep, and try to obtain a vision of that which was ahead of us, he brought me food, water, coals for my pipe, made me comfortable.

'We started out on foot, traveled only in the night-time. We crossed Bear River straight down from Sacred Red Rock,[1] before which we stopped to give it a few presents, and ask it to pity us, to aid us in that which we had set out to do. We crossed Milk River [Teton River] just below the butte for which our far-back fathers named it,[2]

---

[1] A large red rock on the north slope of the Marias River, just above Great Northern Railway Branch, Great Falls to Shelby, and Sweetgrass. The soil upon which it rests is so loose that the rock is gradually moving downhill.
[2] A butte having the appearance of a woman's breast, and a little way east of the town of Chouteau. In Blackfeet, *Onuhkists* (breasts). Milk is *onuhkis*.

and, just below the mouth of Point-of-Rocks River, crossed Big River.[1] Yes, right where now stands that town of many houses [Great Falls], there we stopped that early morning, to rest and sleep until night should come again. Our shelter was a small grove of cottonwoods and willows along the riverbank. We had no meat, and were very hungry that morning. On the plain, well out from us, were several herds of buffalo and antelope. Said one of our party: "If we only had meat of one of them, how safely we could broil it with this smokeless bark." He pointed to the dead, dry bark of a fallen cottonwood.

'Said another: "The animals are all quiet; there seems to be no enemy war party hereabout; let us go out there and make a killing."

' "No. We will take no chances; no risks whatever. Quiet though it seems to be, out there, yet somewhere, hidden from us, a large enemy war party may also be hungrily looking at the herds," I said.

' "We cannot travel without food. As you will not allow us to go out there and make a killing, just you make some of the animals come right in here," said another, Bear Bones, always cross, always complaining, but a brave, successful man of many war trails.

---

[1]Junction of Sun River and the Missouri.

'I will try to bring some of them in," I answered, and had Wolf Plume hand me my medicine-pipe roll. I did not expose the pipe. Simply held the roll up to the sky and prayed Sun, Thunder Bird, and Ancient Raven, to make food come to us.

'We watched the herds; particularly the one nearest us, a small herd of buffalo, all of them save one old cow, lying down and chewing again the grass with which they had filled themselves. The cow was standing with lowered head, motionless, asleep on her feet. But now she raised her head, stretched out her legs, shook herself, and started slowly walking toward us. Up rose the herd then, two or three at first, then all the others, and in single file came on behind her. And I said to the cross one: "There, Bear Bones, as you asked, so have I done with the help of my medicine. And now you do the killing. Not with your gun, but with your silent bow and arrows."

' "Yes," he answered.

'A fat one. A cow without calf, or a one-winter or two-winters one," said I.

' "All of my party were looking at me, thinking that I had great favor with the Above Ones; that my medicine was powerful. I said nothing. I was not proud-feeling. Bear Bones asked us to move back, to leave him alone to make his killing. We went down to the shore of the river. Presently we heard a great pounding and rattling of hoofs; smashing of brush and dead sticks; and some of the herd came running out to the shore, below, and turned and ran up past us and then back through the timber to the plain, all but one, a cow of two winters, with an arrow deep in her side, just back of her shoulder. Right in front of us she fell, blood streaming from her nose and mouth, and died. And came out from the timber Bear Bones, saw her, and said: "Ha! There she lies. I knew that she could not go far with my arrow in her lungs."

'So was it that, by the favor of the Above Ones, we ate fat, broiled meat that morning, and had meat for several days to come. And my companions were happy, eager to go on. That which I had done, my bringing the herd of buffalo to us from the plain, was, they said, a sign that our raid was to be successful. After we finished eating, I went apart from my companions, and, before I slept, smoked and prayed to the Above Ones, and sacrificed to Sun a piece of tobacco from my Thunder Pipe Roll.

'Going on south, night after night, we crossed the Yellow Mountains [Judith Mountains] through the low gap in them, and one morning, just before Sun appeared, arrived at Dried Meat River [Musselshell River]. We crossed it, and stopped in a small grove of timber. We still had meat of the buffalo that Bear Bones had killed; thin cuttings of it, now partly dried. Wolf Plume broiled some of it for me, and, after eating, I had him prepare a resting-place for me, in some thick willows a little farther down the grove, and, after naming two of my companions to go on watch until the middle of the day, I lay down in it, my sacred pipe roll at my side, and soon slept.

'I had a vision. I saw a camp of many lodges; it was night, yet I saw the lodges plainly, and horses tied close to them. And then I saw riders going away from the camp, driving before them a herd of horses. I awoke. Sun was nearing the middle of the blue. I lay there until my helper came and called me, and then joined my companions, all of them up and broiling meat at a little smokeless fire. My helper gave me some meat, and, as I ate, I told my vision. All agreed with me that it was a good one; that its meaning was that we were to have good success and get many horses from an enemy camp somewhere ahead.

'We heard a raven making its hoarse cry. It came from the north and rested upon a branch of a dead tree under which we were sitting.

Again and again it gave its loud hoarse cries, looking down at us, and off to the south. My companions looked up at it, looked at me. As I was a sacred-pipe man, I sang the raven's song: "Wind, it is my element, powerful is the wind."

'And then: "Buffalo I am looking for. I have found them. I have found them upon the ground. The ground is my element. It is powerful."

'The raven listened to my singing, looked down at me, turning its head sideways, looking at me first with one eye, then the other, and when I had finished, it gave four cries, spread its wings, and went flying on to the south. That was another sign that we were to have good luck. We were impatient for the coming of night, so that we could go on southward.

'When the new day came, we arrived at the north end of the Bad Mountains [Crazy Mountains], and stopped at the head of a small river, Bad River [Shields River], that flows down the west side of them, southward into Elk River. Some time before the coming of the next day, we neared the junction of the two rivers, and saw fresh horse tracks in a dusty buffalo trail that we were following. That meant that we were probably near an enemy camp. The far side of Elk River was Crow country. We went up onto a near hill that was well grown over with juniper and other brush, and there awaited the coming of day. It came, and to the south of us, where Elk River comes from the mountains out into the plain, we saw rising the smoke of many lodge fires, of a big Crow camp, of course.

'Leaving me alone on watch on the hill, my companions went down into the timber bordering the river, and built a war lodge of poles and brush, and, when it was completed and a small fire of dry bark burning in it, I went down into it, Wolf Plume taking my place on the hill. I called upon Black Elk to assist me, and together we burned some sweetgrass, purified ourselves in the smoke from it, and, with the prayers and songs belonging to it, went through the complete ceremony of my Thunder Medicine; praying each of us, as the pipe went the round of our circle, for success against the enemy, and safe return to our people. That done, we rested there for the remainder of the day, keeping good watch upon the country from the hilltop, but failing to see any enemies anywhere about. There were plenty of buffalo between us and Elk River; more herds of them on the other side of it. The Crows, we thought, must be making their killings of meat very near their camp.

'Came night, and we went on down to Elk River, built a raft of driftwood, placed upon it our weapons, clothing, and various belongings, sacrificed to the underwater people some small presents, praying them that we might safely cross their element, and so took to the water, holding onto our raft and swimming. We easily made the other shore, some distance downstream, dressed, and went on, following up the valley of the river. Morning had not come when we heard, far ahead of us, the dogs of the camp answering the howling of the wolves about it. We did not want to go on and raid the camp; we wanted first to see it, see how the people cared for their horses, and how we could best get some of them. We therefore went up onto the slope of the valley, where was plenty of cover, small pines and juniper brush, there to remain until night should come again.

'Day came and revealed to us that which made our hearts glad: A little way farther up the valley, in a wide, grassed flat and near heavy timber bordering the river, was a circle of more than two hundred lodges. Lodges of new, white leather; whitely gleaming in the light of rising Sun. And tethered close to the lodges of their owners were many horses; the war horses, the fast, trained buffalo horses of which their owners were so proud. Other horses there were, many, many bands of them, grazing in the great bottom above, below, and out around the camp. Smoke was rising from the lodges; women were hurrying to the river for water; to the timber for fuel; men were going, some of them to bathe, others were caring for their horses: they were rich, powerful people, our enemies, the Crows.

'Said Bear Bones: "It will be easy to take all of those far-out grazing horses that we can drive, but I don't want them. I want, I am going to have, some of those big, powerful, swift ones that are tied here and there in the camp."

'So said all the others of our party.

'In all that great camp, there was but one painted lodge; the Crows seemed to have few sacred-pipe men; anyhow, there was but this one lodge that had sacred paintings upon it. A very large lodge it was, and well apart from the others, in the lower side of the circle. Two black-and-white spotted horses were tied in front of its doorway. Pointing to them, I said to my companions: "Those two there in front of the painted lodge, they are mine."

"Yes. Yours, the two spotted ones," they answered.

'Just then a man came out of the painted lodge, untied the two horses, smoothed their manes and tails with a handful of brush, then led them to the river to drink. Presently he brought them back into the open, hobbled one and let it go, led the other back to his lodge, and saddled it. Many other men were saddling their swift animals; they were going out to run buffalo. I prayed to my medicine, to the Above Ones. "Pity me; help me. Let this be the last time that painted lodge man will ride that spotted fast one. Help me to take it and its spotted mate," I said.

'Sun was but a little way up in the blue when a hundred or more riders gathered at the lower side of the camp circle, and came down the valley, went down past us, talking, laughing, singing, happy all of them. And following them were their women, with travois horses and pack-horses, for bringing in the meat and hides of the killing that was to be made.

'I named two to remain on watch, and we others lay down and slept. Came the middle of the day, and we sat up, and the two lay down. I wanted no more sleep that day. I was uneasy. We had dangerous work to do, and my companions looked to me as well as to their own sacred helpers for protection in it. True, my visions had been favorable, but I could not be sure that we should not, some of us, get into trouble. I prayed again and again to the Above Ones. I promised Sun that, provided we survived our raid that night, my woman would build for him a sacred lodge.

'The day was hot, and we became very thirsty; but in going up onto the valley slope to watch the camp, we thought we were to suffer from want of water. We had food, dried meat, but dared not eat of it, for that would make us still more thirsty. Idly we watched the big camp; men visiting one another, sitting out in the shade of the lodges, talking, smoking; women busy tanning robes, and leather; children playing everywhere about. We knew that there were a few women of our own kind down there, women whom the Crows had captured many winters back when a large war party of them had ambushed a number of our hunters out after buffalo, on Yellow River. We wondered if they were happy; contented. Black Elk said that they probably had become Crows in all but their blood. Had we not in our tribe Crow women, Snake women, Kûtenai women, Cree women, and women of the West-Side tribes, whom our warriors had captured, and with their children, plenty of food, good clothes, were they not happy? Yes. They had even said, many of them, that they would rather die than return to their own kind. And there was Painted Wing's woman, Pine Tree Woman;

she went with him to war against her own people, the West-Side, River People.

'Said my young helper, Wolf Plume: "I am so poor that none of the girls of our tribe will so much as look at me, so I will try to capture one of the girls down there. It is said that the Crow girls are very beautiful."

'You will make no attempt of that kind this night. You are to stand in that point of timber there below the camp, and take care of the horses that we bring to you," I told him.

'You know that I was but making nothing-talk," he answered.

'Sun was not far above the mountains when the Crow hunters came riding back up the valley, their women trailing after them with their travois horses and pack-horses drawing and carrying big loads of meat and hides. Again the men were singing happily; their women, too. I watched my spotted horse and its rider. The man was short and slender. The horse seemed not to be tired, for now and then he pranced; trotted sideways.

'I said to my companions: "See my beautiful spotted horse. See him prance. He is not tired, he, my spotted horse."

' "But after being used all day, and tied again for the night, he will have little strength for the long, fast run we will have to make," said one.

'Ah! But the rider is going to let him graze until night," I answered.

'Ha! Arrived at his lodge, the rider unsaddled the spotted one, hobbled him and turned him out to grass. Yes. As I willed the rider should do, so did he.

'I said to my companions: "My friends, very powerful is my sacred medicine."

' "Ah! Powerful! Powerful!" they repeated.

'Sun went to his island home. Night came, and we sneaked down into the valley and through the timber to the river, and drank plenty of water and ate of our dried meat. I then led my companions to the point of timber, a little way below the camp, that I had selected for our gathering-place, and there we remained until visiting, feasting, smoking, dancing, and singing in the big camp ceased, until the lodge fires all died out and the people slept. I then told Wolf Plume to watch for our return to the point with horses, and again advised my companions to be very cautious in approaching and entering the camp, and to go into it separately, in its north, south, and east sides. We then left the point and soon lost sight of one another in the darkness.

'The night could not have been better for our raid; clouds hid Night-Light, above us, yet it was not too dark; we could see objects, make out what they were, at a distance of twenty or twenty-five steps. So was it that I surely but slowly approached the big painted lodge. To go to it, I had to pass between two lodges at the outer edge of the circle. When quite near them, I stopped, listened, heard in one of them the heavy breathing of a sleeper. I went on, and made out that a dark object that I was approaching was a horse; and then I saw that it was one of my black-and-white spotted buffalo runners. It did not flinch from me when I went right to it and stroked its shoulder. Its rope, I made out, was fastened to a peg of the lodge skin. I stood beside the horse, looking, listening. All was quiet. I believed that I knew where my other spotted one was tied. I went on past the doorway of the lodge and right to it, its rope end fastened also to a lodge peg. I noiselessly untied it, coiled it as I moved on to the horse, and then started leading him to the other one. But slowly; only a step or two at a time. When I had got right in front of the lodge, a sleeper within began dream-talking; not loud; a few words at a time. But I didn't like that; people who talk in their sleep wake up. This one might awake, hear the horses moving off, and come out. I was very uneasy; led the horse still more slowly;

and at last came to the other one; and his rope I cut, at right length for leading him, and then I went on with the two, backing away from the painted lodge until I could no longer see it, then watching the two other lodges as I passed between them; on out from the camp and at faster pace to the point of timber. Several of my companions had already arrived there with their takings of horses, and had gone again for more of them. Wolf Plume took charge of mine, and said: "Ha! The two spotted ones. You said, up there on the valley slope, that they were yours, and you spoke the truth; they are yours."

' "Yes. And now I go to the camp for more of them," I answered.

' "Wait. Hear me. Pity me, Sun-Power man," said he. "I have worked for you, carried your medicine things; do pity me; let me go at least once into this enemy camp and take horses, even one horse. I want to be a warrior. I want to be able to count at least one *coup* when, this summer, we build Sun's great lodge."

' "Yes, I do pity you," I answered. "When I come again, I will make some one take your place here, and you shall go into the camp with me."

'Again I led two horses to the meeting-place, and close following me came Bear Bones with three, making five that he had taken. I asked him to remain there until Wolf Plume could make one entrance into the camp with me. He objected; said that he had not come with me as a servant.

' "You were once as is this youth; anxious to count your first *coup*. Some one did for you as I now ask you to do for him," I answered.

' "True. Go, you two. I will watch our takings here," he said.

'I believed that my companions had none of them been in the upper part of the big camp, so I decided that we would try our luck up there. With Wolf Plume close at my side, and moving slowly, noiselessly, I passed between the two lodges just below the painted lodge, went by it and two others, and was then in the grass and sagebrush bottom land that the circle of the lodges enclosed. It was maybe two hundred steps across. We were nearing the lodges at its upper side, were rounding an almost shoulder-high patch of sagebrush, when a man rose up close in front of us and spoke three or four words, no doubt asking who we were or where we were going. He never spoke again nor even groaned; I struck the top of his head with the end of my rifle barrel, and with all my strength, and he dropped, and Wolf Plume, who carried no gun, only bow and arrows in the case upon his back, gave a downward spring and stabbed him in his breast; and then whispered to me: "Here. Take my knife and scalp him."

' "I will take one side, you the other," I answered; and when we had done that, we felt about for any weapons that the dead one might have had, but could find none; not even a knife in his belt. He was not a night watcher for the camp, else he would have had a gun or bow and arrows. He had recently come from his lodge for one purpose or another, had probably awakened his woman when leaving his couch, and she would become alarmed if he did not soon return to her, and would arouse the camp. I whispered to Wolf Plume that we must go on.

'We soon came to the lodges in the upper part of the circle and found that there were horses tied before all of them. We each took two, from lodges at the outer edge of the circle, and led them well out toward the edge of the bottom, and thence down to the meeting-place. Besides Bear Bones, four others were there with second and third takings, and close after us came in the rest, with one, and two, and even three more horses each.

'Said Bear Bones: "I thought that you two would never return. Now I go again for more."

' "No. With the takings that we have, we start for home right now," I answered.

' "No. I want more of these Crow horses." "So do I," said several others.

' "We cannot go into the camp again. We have killed a man; he will be missed; the whole camp will soon be called upon to look for him," I explained, but even then Bear Bones was strong for us to raid the camp again. All the others sided with me, however, and he had to give in.

' "True, we have not taken many horses, but those that we have are every one of the fast buffalo runners, fast and powerful war horses; better these few than a big herd of those slower ones, grazing out there in the bottom."

'Mounting each of us one of our takings, I led off, the others driving the loose horses after me; and we were not out of the bottom when we heard great shouting and crying back in that enemy camp. At that, we went on with all the speed that we could make with our little band of loose animals. But that, we felt, was fast enough, for we could frequently change on to fresh horses, and so outride any who might pursue us. Three times we so changed before we came to Elk River, and twice more after crossing it. And if any of the

Crows did take our trail, we never saw them. We made the long way back to our people without trouble, and got great praise for our success. Yes, and one of the Sun lodge-builders of that summer was my woman.

'Kyi! I end my tale.'

CHAPTER XI

STRONG MEDICINE

ONE evening in our Waterton Lakes Park camp, when a number of guests of the big hotel came to sit with us around our lodge fire and listen to our talk — interpreted to them, of course — I said to old Ahkó Mûkstokîks (Many Big Ears, Blackfeet name for mules), 'Old friend, it is now for you to tell of your fighting days.'

'To-night, why not something different?' he queried. 'So far, all our talk here has been of war. Oh, I went against enemy tribes many times, counted *coups* on two Crees, two Kalispels, one Assiniboin, one Crow, that I killed on different raids; stole many horses, and one woman, a woman of the River People. But somehow I don't feel like talking of all that, to-night. It is this that has been in my thoughts all day, and I think that it will interest you:

'Very long ago, before we obtained horses, when we used dogs to draw and to carry our belongings, there came a time when our Ka´ina [Blood] tribe made a peace agreement with the Crees. For several winters after that, members of the two tribes frequently visited one another.

'Came to the Ka'ina camp, one day, a number of Cree visitors, and were welcomed in the lodges of their friends. One of the Crees, a big, fine-appearing man, visiting here and there in the camp, saw a very beautiful young woman, and wanted her, although back in the camp of his own people he had three women. He began following this young woman about, and at last, getting a chance to speak to her out of hearing of others, he asked her to go with him to his camp, become his woman. That made her very angry; she called him a dog face; told him to go away and never again speak to her. He laughed, told her that she would become his woman later on.

'Some days after this, the young woman was out with others, picking berries, when the Cree suddenly ran in among them and seized her and made her run off with him, threatening to stab her with his big flint knife if she held back. The other women hurried in to camp and told of her seizure by the Cree. Her man was out hunting; she had no near relatives; the visiting Crees said that the one who had stolen her was a very dangerous man, for he had a medicine that enabled him to kill people without striking them himself. So was it that none attempted to trail the stealer and rescue the woman.

'The woman's man, Big Elk, did not return from his hunt until the following day. And upon learning that the Cree had stolen his woman, he became very angry. Were all the men of his tribe cowards, that they did not run after the thief and kill him? he asked. Well, he himself was no coward. What if the thief did have a powerful medicine? He was going right to the Cree camp and take his woman. Yes, there were others who had a powerful medicine. He had one. He would soon learn which was the more powerful of the two.

'Two days later, Big Elk entered the Cree camp, went to the chief of the tribe, and complained of the thief; asked for help in recovering his woman. The chief replied that the man had a medicine so powerful that none dared anger him.

' "I will see how powerful he is. Which of these is his lodge?"

'The chief pointed to it. Big Elk went quickly to it, entered, sat down just inside the doorway. On the women's side of the lodge was his woman. Upon his couch in the rear of the lodge, sat the thief.

' "My woman, I have come for you," said Big Elk. His woman made no reply to that; she was crying; she held out her hands to him, but at once dropped them in her lap when the thief shouted to Big Elk:

' "You can't have the woman. You go from my lodge at once."

' "I will go from it with my woman. I have come for her. I shall have her," Big Elk replied.

' "Never again will she be your woman. She is mine. I shall keep her. And now I tell you this: leave my lodge at once, return to your people, or you shall die right here. I have a powerful medicine; I shall cause it to kill you, right there where you sit, if you do not do as I say," shouted the Cree.

' "Try it. I am not afraid of your medicine."

' "Twice, now, I have told you to leave my lodge. Again I tell you, go, or suffer a terrible death."

'Big Elk made no answer to that; just sat and stared at the Cree.

'Said the Cree: "Again, and for the last time, I tell you to leave my lodge at once."

'No reply.

'That was the fourth time that he had been ordered to leave the lodge, and he knew, did Big Elk, that the Cree would now attempt to carry out his threat. But still he did not move, just sat there motionless staring straight into his enemy's eyes.

'The Cree took from the head of his couch a quill-embroidered, red-painted sack, opened it, brought out a small image of a man, set it upright upon the ground, and said to Big Elk: "There he is, my powerful medicine. He will go over to you, kill you right there where you sit."

' "Good. Tell him to come."

'The Cree spoke to the image, and it started walking around the fireplace and toward Big Elk. And said the Cree: "Your end is near; when he reaches you, he will kill you."

' "Never will he get me," said Big Elk, and brought out his own medicine, an image of a spider; made of soft deer leather, embroidered with quills of various colors. He prayed to it, a short little prayer, set it upon the ground, and it started running toward the man image; got near it, cast an end of its body thread around the neck of the image, then ran across the lodge and to a pole, and up it, trailing its body thread as it went. Then, when well up the pole, it began to draw in the thread, and soon the noosed image was pulled from the ground, slowly was drawn up, higher and higher, nearer to the drawer, the spider image.

The women cried out at this strange sight, and the Cree thief stared at his medicine image with eyes of fear.

'Then said Big Elk to the thief: "Your medicine that you said was so powerful, it is worthless, a nothing-medicine. When my spider draws it all the way up, seizes and bites it into small pieces, then do you die, right there where you sit."

'The thief stared at Big Elk with fear, his lips trembled; he held out trembling hands and cried: "Pity me. Do not let your spider seize my little man. I give you back your woman; take her and go."

'Big Elk made no answer to that. He sat there smiling, singing very softly the song of his spider image. The man image rose higher and higher, twirling this way, that way, and when it was but a little way from the spider image, the Cree thief began to cry, and whimpered to Big Elk: "Do not let your spider draw my man any higher. I give not only your woman; I also give you my weasel-skin war shirt, my eagle-tail-feathered war bonnet, my weapons, all else of mine that you may like. Pity me, great chief, allow me to live."

' "Your medicine, then, is a useless medicine, without power?"

' "Just that; powerless. Pity me. Let me live."

'Big Elk laughed. Spoke to his spider image, and it let the man image drop to the ground, and there it lay, the Cree thief nor his women paying any attention to it. The spider descended the pole, walked over to Big Elk, and he took it up and put it back in his medicine sack. And then said to the Cree: "I want two of your dogs with the travois that they draw. Load upon the travois your war clothes, and the other things that you gave me; also some food, and several good robes. Do this; have your women do it quickly, if you want to live."

'The thief spoke to his women; they hurried to get the dogs and travois, and loaded them with the valuable things. When that was done, Big Elk said to the Cree: "Well, we go, my woman and I. Come again to my camp and steal her. Come soon."

'And with that, the two left the lodge, and, leading the dogs, went their homeward way.'

CHAPTER XII

MANY BIG EARS' PICTOGRAPHS

IT was our last evening in our Waterton Lake camp, and we were all gathered around the little fire in Weasel Tail's lodge. As his big pipe was going the round of our circle, he said to Many Big Ears: 'That "Strong Medicine" story you told us, the other night, was good. But before we break camp, we think we should have a war story from you. Tell of that time when the Crows surrounded you, and you got away from them, and show us the painting that you have made of it.'

Many Big Ears had his wife hand him a large, square piece of buffalo leather upon which, in blue, red, yellow, and black, were his pictographs of his encounter with the Crows, and lower down, others of an angry buffalo bull that he had once met and killed.

'We were a very small party; only five of us,' he began. 'From the big camp of our people, then on Bow River, we went south to raid the

Crows. After traveling many nights, we at last found a Crow camp on Bighorn River, a little way up it from its junction with Elk River [the Yellowstone]. Night-Light was showing all of herself; we could see almost as well as though it were day. We separated, went into camp to take the good buffalo horses and war horses that were tied close to the lodges of their owners. I got four of them out without arousing the sleeping people, and, when a little way from the camp circle, mounted one of them, and, leading the others, started for the place down the valley where I was to meet my companions. Ha! I had gone but a little way when I came almost face to face with six riders, and one of them spoke to me, and I knew that he was a Crow. No doubt he said, "Who are you?" For answer, I aimed my rifle at him and pulled the trigger, but there was only the click of the hammer; the cap was a bad one. At that, I let go the ropes of the three horses I was leading, and rode as fast as possible for the timber bordering the river, the six Crows after me, and shooting at me. At the edge of a big patch of willows, I sprang from the horses and ran into the willows, and my enemies surrounded it, firing into it, yelling loudly, and so awakened the people in the big camp, and many of them came running, eager to fight. I thought that they would soon have my scalp, but, anyhow, I prayed to the Above Ones, to my sacred helper, to help me in some way to survive.

'Ha! Before the men from the camp arrived, one of the six set fire to the willow patch. It was in the time of falling leaves; the grass in the willows was brown and dry; many of the willows were dead and dry. The fire burned fiercely. I prayed still harder for help, and got it. A very strong wind suddenly sprang up, blowing across the valley and toward the river, and causing the fire to make a very thick, black smoke. I went with the smoke, as noiselessly as possible, but choking, eyes smarting so that I was almost blinded. But I kept on, and, without being seen by any of the enemy, stumbled down a steep bank and into the river, which was not deep; and, still concealed in the black smoke, I crossed to the other side, and went down the valley, keeping in the timber and brush as much as possible, and so at last was safe. And I kept going; crossed Elk River before daylight, and remained in a grove until night, when I went on again. I saw nothing of my companions. I traveled night after night until I arrived at Many Houses [Fort Benton], and had help again, for the Pikû´ni were encamped there, and one, a close friend, gave me a horse, and I rode back to Bow River and my people.

'So, you see, here is my painting of it; I am standing in a circle, which means that I am surrounded, and the lone branch running up from the top of the circle shows that I am in a patch of willows. The men surrounding the circle and shooting are, of course, the Crows.

'Again, these lower paintings are about the meanest buffalo bull that I ever met. They show just what happened. The big camp of us was at the west butte of the Sweetgrass Hills, and one day my father and I went over on Little River [Milk River] to hunt. We separated, he riding up the north side, and I the south side of the valley. We had gone up but a little way when I saw a lone buffalo bull coming to water; running swiftly down the slope of the valley, to arrive at the river quite a little way above me. He made me think of one of the sacred songs of the Beaver Medicine, the Buffalo Bull song: "When I go to water, I run." I sang it. I knew that I had no right to do that, but I happened to have, that morning, an "I-don't-care-feeling," so sang it anyhow. And what do you think happened then? Lone Buffalo Bull heard that song; it made him angry; he swerved from the way he was going, and came straight at me. I fired at his head, but that didn't stop him. I turned my horse to run away from him, but he struck the animal in the rear, knocking him over, and me off, and badly tore one of the horse's legs. And with that, the bull went on to the river and began drinking. I was then angry. I fired at the bull again, and the bullet went into his shoulder; he staggered from the river and fell. I ran to him, severed the cords of his hind legs, and told him to get upon his feet and fight me. He tried to get up; shook his head at me; his eyes were like fire. My father came over and stabbed him in the heart. So died he, that mean bull.'

And now, a few remarks about Indian pictographs.

The pictographs that the Blackfeet tribes artists draw of animals, and particularly those on sacred lodges, such as the buffalo, beaver, and otter, are drawn with the so-called life-line; a line running from the mouth down the neck and back to nearly the center of the body, where it ends in a triangular figure, representing the heart. Of the Northwest Algonquian tribes, the Blackfeet alone draw the life-line, and we wonder where they got the idea.

We once saw a reproduction of a photograph of a pictograph from an excavation in a village of the prehistoric 'Mound-Builders,' of the Mississippi Valley. The pictograph was that of a deer, was cut into a shoulder blade of a deer, and in it was the life-line, ending in a representation of the heart.

We should like some anthropologist to work out the connection between that ancient drawing and those of the Blackfeet tribes.

CHAPTER XIII

CHIEF CROWFOOT

WHILE we were with the Blackfeet, recording their sacred tobacco rites, several of our old friends asked us to be sure to include in our writing mention of their dead and gone chief, Isapwo´ Muksika (Crow Big-Foot), or as the whites understood his name, Crowfoot. Said Old Bull, 'You know as well as we do, that he was the greatest chief of all three tribes of us.'

The Blackfeet are not alone in that opinion of the chief. The Canadians thought so highly of him that their Government has erected a fine monument in memory of his sterling worth, and on the brow of a hill overlooking the Blackfeet Crossing of Bow River, where he gathered the tribes together and induced them to sign a treaty which the Government was very anxious to make with them. And a little farther down the rim of the valley is a neat circle of cemented stonework, thirty feet in diameter, and in the center of it a tablet, setting forth that here Chief Crowfoot made his last camp, and died.

Crowfoot was born in 1830, and his boyhood was uneventful. When he became old enough to go to war, he had a strange vision; there came to him in his lone and long fast, in which he sought a sacred helper, a strange being who announced that he was a buffalo-man, and would be his helper. And among other things, he told him, Crowfoot, that he was become chief, more by doing good to and for his own people than by war records which he would make. Thereafter, he always wore a pair of buffalo calf leggings, as the symbol of his vision.

After Crowfoot had been upon several raids against his enemy, his elders attained so much confidence in him that they made him a scout, and a little later often sought his advice in planning an attack upon the camp of an enemy. Still later, when he announced that he was going to make an enemy raid, older warriors were eager to go with him, so assured were they of his bravery and his discretion. In time, he made for himself a fine record of successes against the enemy. And then he began listening to the talk and the advice of his white friends. They said that the buffalo were going, would soon be exterminated; that many white people would come from the East to turn the buffalo plains into fields of wheat and hay for cattle. They advised Crowfoot to urge his people to do likewise. He replied that the time had not come for that for his buffalo-hunting kindred; so long as there were any buffalo, they would hunt them; that when they could no longer hunt, he would then do his best to make farmers of them.

Then came the matter of a treaty with the Blackfeet, Bloods, and North Pikû´ni, which the Government was very anxious to have ratified; the famous treaty of 1877. With the wide influence that he had, Crowfoot got the tribes together at Blackfeet Crossing, and urged them to sign the treaty for their own good. They held back for a long time, but he finally had his way with them, and was the first one of them all to sign it.

In the summer of 1880, Crowfoot led his people to buffalo for, as it proved, their last great hunt of the animals. As they had agreed to do, they came to the Missouri River–Musselshell River country to winter, and trade with us at our post on the Missouri, about thirty miles above the mouth of the Musselshell. Neither they nor we knew that, desperate from want of food, a thousand and more Canadian Crees, under their chief, Big Bear, were also coming there to hunt. Come they did, deadly enemies of the Blackfeet, and Crowfoot went out and met Big Bear and had a long talk with him. The result of it was that the two tribes went into camp side by side, and that they never quarreled with one another; for the two chiefs, going arm in arm through both camps, loudly proclaimed that they two together would put to death any and all who did not keep the peace.

Came there, a little later, Riel and his band of Red River mixed bloods, and there hatched the plot against the Canadian Government that was to be the Riel Rebellion, in 1883. My partner, the late Joseph Kipp, and I, and, too, a certain Jesuit priest who was with us, Father Scullins, did our best to show Riel that the proposed out-break was without any justification whatever, and that it was sure to fail, but he and his underchiefs only laughed at us and called us fools. Big Bear and his Crees eagerly agreed to join the Red Rivers — French Crees, the most of them — and fight the Red Coats to the bitter end. But Crow-foot would have nothing to do with them. The Red Coats were his good friends; their Great Mother was his Great Mother, too. He and his warriors would never fight them. However, many of the young men of his tribe said that, when the time came, they would go in with the Red Rivers and the

Crees against the whites; and at that, Riel went to Crowfoot, and said that, as so many of his, Crowfoot's, young warriors were to join his forces, it would be the wise thing for him to lead them; if he didn't, his tribe would call him an old woman, and some one else would become chief of the Blackfeet.

Said Crowfoot in reply: 'You, Worthless White Man-Cree: So long as I live, I shall be chief of my people! And I tell you right now that not one of them will ever fight with you against my Red Coat friends!'

In the summer of 1882, Crowfoot and his children, as he called them, turned their backs upon the few remaining buffalo herds, between the Missouri and the Yellowstone, and returned to their Alberta reservation, never again to roam the buffalo plains. Came the spring of 1883, and Riel launched his rebellion against the Red Coats. Some of the young Blackfeet warriors, and a number of those of the Blood tribe, became restless, wanted to join Riel's forces, but Crowfoot held them back with an iron hand. The Canadian Government became very uneasy as to the attitude of these two tribes, and one day, when Crowfoot was traveling about among his people, sternly admonishing the younger men that they were to have no part in the rebellion, a mounted policeman brought him a message from his friend, Apopi, General Strange. 'Will my friend, Crowfoot, be able to keep his young men at home in peace and order?' he asked. 'If not, I will go with my troops to his assistance, instead of proceeding North.'

'You tell him to go North. I have my young men in hand. Not one of them will join the Crees,' he replied.

Crowfoot's remaining years were devoted to encouraging his children to follow the white men's trail; to plant ever-increasing acreages of wheat, and enlarge their herds of cattle. As a result of that, they are to-day a most prosperous tribe of Indians, harvesting annually something like $200,000 worth of wheat; not even drawing the interest on their funds in the Interior Department of their Government; for the very good reason that they do not need it.

Crowfoot died in 1890, his passing mourned by all his kind, and a host of white friends, too.

And so, as our old Blood and Blackfeet friends would say:

Kyi! It is finished. We end our tale!

THE END

ABOUT THE AUTHORS

JAMES WILLARD SCHULTZ
and JESSIE LOUISE DONALDSON

James Willard Schultz was born in Boonville, New York, in 1859. His upper-class family harbored hopes that he would follow in its footsteps into genteel society, but at a young age James amply demonstrated that his rebellious and adventurous predilections would lead him down a different path. Schoolrooms and book learning held little attraction for Schultz, who preferred the freedom of roaming the Adirondacks on hunting and camping trips under the tutelage of guides hired by his family. Thinking that James's fondness for the rough life in the woods and an interest in firearms presaged a military career, his family packed him off to Peekskill Military Academy on the Hudson in anticipation of his entering West Point.

An 1877 trip to his uncle's hotel in St. Louis, Missouri, however, altered Schultz's destiny. At the Planters Hotel in St. Louis, he encountered Indian fur traders, roustabouts, hide hunters, steamboat pilots, and other frontiersmen from the upper Missouri River country. They plied him with vivid stories of life among the Indians—which so fired his imagination that he soon booked passage to Fort Benton, Montana, on the steamboat *Far West*.

Using letters of introduction, James fortuitously connected with Joseph Kipp, a fur trader with the Piegan Blackfeet, and worked with Kipp for several years. Schultz married a Blackfeet woman named Natahki (Fine Shield Woman) in 1879 and participated in the tribe's final years of following the buffalo herds. He was allowed the rare privilege of joining the Piegan in their religious ceremonies, and he turned his keen ear to the tribal leaders and warriors as they retold their deeds of valor and adventure. Schultz was given the name "APikû´ni " by the Pikû´ni chief, Running Crane. APikû´ni in Blackfoot means Spotted Robe.

When the buffalo herds were exterminated from the northern plains in the early 1880s, Schultz and Natahki settled down on a simple ranch on the Blackfeet reservation. From 1886 to 1903 they raised livestock and guided hunting parties into the mountains to the west (the area now known as Glacier National Park).

Schultz supplemented their income by writing articles for national newspapers and magazines. George Bird Grinnell, editor of *Forest and Stream*, was one of Schultz's hunting clients and was particularly impressed with Schultz's narration of frontier experiences. A life-long friendship ensued between the two to their mutual benefit.

Natahki died of a heart ailment in 1903, and not long afterwards Schultz became involved in a hunting violation with the son of the famous journalist Joseph Pulitzer. When the violation was discovered, Pulitzer's son was apprehended and convicted, and Schultz fled the state to avoid arrest. He eventually settled in California, where he worked first for an oil company and then a newspaper. He married Celia Belle Hawkins in 1907 and divorced in 1930, reportedly an unhappy union.

During this unsettled period of his life, he penned his first—and perhaps finest—book length manuscript, *My Life as an Indian*. Its success began a long writing career. Between 1907 and 1940 Schultz produced thirty-seven titles celebrating Indian life on the frontier. Schultz's writing forte was conjuring dialogue and plot in a manner that wove authenticity into a fascinating story. Some books were entirely fictional and others were honest attempts to record oral traditions and events as narrated by his Blackfeet friends. Many books were aimed at young readers, and with millions of young Americans reading his books, he became one of the country's foremost interpreters of Indian culture.

Historians object to Schultz's writings as factually unreliable because of Schultz's occasional inability to attribute correct dates, places, and participants to events that happened decades prior to the writing. Schultz never claimed to be a scholarly historian. His sources were the words of his informants and his own memory.

Despite the occasional inaccuracy, Schultz's first-hand accounts of late nineteenth century Blackfeet cultural practices and folklore are without peer. William J. Long, author of *American Literature*, wrote of Schultz in 1941: "Of all our writers, early and late, he is the only one who comes near to knowing the soul of an Indian."

In 1931 Schultz married Jessie Louise Donaldson, an anthropologist and English professor at Montana State University. He had met her in 1927 and prior to their marriage she collaborated with him on *The Sun God's Children*. During the Great Depression they lived on the Blackfeet Reservation where she began a program to revive Blackfeet craft skills. She summarized Schultz's work well: "His close observations of Indian life in many instances are excellent ethnographic accounts. Reading Schultz for this detail gives us a picture of Blackfeet life that is unobtainable elsewhere."

The Blackfeet agreed. Schultz died in 1947 at the age of eighty-eight and was buried by the Blackfeet in Two Medicine Valley, in the old burial ground of the family of Natahki, his first wife.

THE BLACKFEET TODAY

The Nizitapi, or Real People, as they call each other, were people of the buffalo. They originated on the plains of today's southern Alberta, western Saskatchewan, and central Montana. Today, the tribe resides on the Blackfeet Indian Reservation in Montana, adjacent to Glacier National Park.

The Blackfeet belong to a confederacy that originally included the Blood, North Piegan, and Siksika tribes of Alberta and the Small Robes, a southern band. In the mid-1830s the confederacy's population was estimated at 16,000 to 20,000 members. Artist George Catlin called the Blackfeet "the most powerful tribe of Indians on the continent." In 1837, a smallpox pandemic decimated the confederacy along with other plains tribes.

In 1896, at the urging of George Bird Grinnell, the Blackfeet tribe, then reduced to 1,400 members, signed a $1.5-million agreement with the federal government relinquishing its western territory. The relinquished area later became Glacier National Park.

The name Blackfoot or Blackfeet is an English term. In tribal language, the name is Amskapi Pikûní. *Pikû'ni* derives from an old form meaning, "spotted robes." Occasionally, elders will use *Sokeetapi*, or "Prairie People," and *A Pikû'ni puyi*, "Speakers of the Same Language," as descriptive names.

The Blackfeet Indian Reservation consists of mountains and foothills, lakes and rivers, falling eastward onto the plains. The 1.5-million acre reserve is but a portion of the 26-million-acre tribal homeland recognized by the federal government in 1855. About half of the 15,000 tribal members live on the reservation. Tribal headquarters are located at the Blackfoot Indian Agency in Browning, Montana. Today the Blackfeet are revitalizing their tribal language, culture, and identity in the belief that strength comes from a healthy self-image.

More information about the Blackfeet can be obtained from the following:

Blackfeet Tribe
P.O. Box 850
Browning, MT 59417
Phone: (406) 338-7521/7522
www.blackfeetnation.com

Piegan Institute
P.O. Box 909
Browning, MT 59417
Phone 406-338-3518
www.pieganinstitute.org

Museum of the Plains Indian
P.O. Box 410
Browning, MT 59417
Phone: 406-338-2230

THE MUSEUM OF THE ROCKIES

The Museum of the Rockies inspires visitors to explore the rich natural and cultural history of America's Northern Rocky Mountains. In partnership with Montana State University, the museum reaches diverse communities with engaging exhibits, educational programs and original research that advances public understanding of the collections.

Museum of the Rockies permanent exhibits include a changing exhibit program, dinosaurs, local history (including Native American history), Yellowstone National Park Children's Discovery area, Tinsley Living History Farm (summer only), and the Taylor Planetarium. Admission is free to members. The Museum of the Rockies is located at 600 West Kagy Boulevard in Bozeman, Montana. For more information call 406-994-3466 or visit www.museumoftherockies.org.

This edition of The Sun God's Children *was published in cooperation with the Museum of the Rockies.*

More Native American History Titles

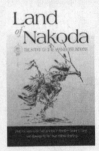